STUDENTS WITH LEARNING DISABILITIES

AT GRADUATE AND PROFESSIONAL

SCHOOL: A PROGRAM AND

STRATEGIES FOR SUCCESS

STUDENTS WITH LEARNING DISABILITIES AT GRADUATE AND PROFESSIONAL SCHOOL: A PROGRAM AND STRATEGIES FOR SUCCESS

✳ ✳ ✳ ✳ ✳

Stanley J. Antonoff, DDS

ISBN   0-89214-055-0

Printed in the United States of America
First Edition

THIS TEXT IS DEDICATED TO ALL THOSE

WHO THROUGH DAILY PERSEVERENCE

HAVE TRIUMPHED OVER THE

CHALLENGES

OF THEIR LEARNING DISABILITIES

CONTRIBUTORS

I am indebted to those contributors listed below whose generosity allows me to endow a rich legacy for the future.

Dr. H. Lee Adamo
Aim Dental Laboratory
      Israel Levin
Sarah Altman
Charles M. Antonoff
Iris Antonoff
Dr. Kenneth & Ruth Antonoff
Dr. Lisa R. Antonoff
Stanley Antonoff
Steven & Rosemarie Antonoff
Sarah N. Arkin
Drs. Lloyd & Mandy Bauer
Morris & Linda Baumstein
Frances Berardi
Drs. Stephen & Juliet Bergen
Beverly Hills Jewish Center
      Sandi Flatow
Dr. Ronald Biondo
Bernice Blatt
Allan & Sally Bloostein
Joel & Susan Bronstein
Lawrence & Susan Buchwalter
Dr. John S. Cavallaro, Sr.
Dr. Vincent & Christine Celenza
William & Nancy Chiswick
Ronald & Sandi Cohen
David & Nina Craighead
Donald & Phyllis Creedman
Dr. Greg Diamond
David & Geraldine DeWitt

Dr. Christopher Duffy
Barbara Estrin
Dr. Mark D. Fili
Barry Finch
Tom & Marlene Foster
Milton & Gertrude Geller
Dr. Igor Gerzon
Dr. Gary R. Goldstein
Walter & Claudine Goodseal
Leonard & Sandi Gubar
Charles & Mafalda Henry
Dr. Paul & Laurel Hoffman
Dr. Edward & Ruth Kaufman
Kildonan School
      Ron Wilson
Michael & Doris Kliegman
Peter & Mona Kliegman
Dr. Irwin Kolin
John D. Kousi
Dr. Peter Koutros
Dr. Lloyd & Jeanette Landa
Dr. Gene & Eleanor Lasota
Dr. Robert Lew
Dr. Harold & Sheila Litvak
Jim & Bernadette Loesch
Walter & Louise Luffsey
Dr. Norman & Margaret Margolin
Raymond & Jean Martin
Leroy & Sonia Mersal
Dr. Robert & Virginia Miner

Dr. Dennis & Margo Morea
Austin S. Moscowitz
Drs. Steven & Marci Moss
Barbara B. Neurohr
New York Branch, IDA
    Linda Selvin
Robert & Gail Peck
Dr. Chris Philip
Dr. Robert & Joyce Pickering
Patrick & Simone Purcell
Dr. Jennifer Rawlins
Barry & Nancy Riebau
Heidi A. Renner
Martin & Marilyn Roberts
Max & Julia Rockoff
Dr. Ed Rosenthal
Dr. Steven & Doris Rubin
Dr. Robert & Maureen Saporito
Dr. Francis & Adeline Sarro, Jr.
Dr. Robert & Rose Schweitzer
Joan Sedita
Daniel & Judith Sennett
Bud & Jean Shadle
Jack & Rhonda Siegel
Alvin & Marilyn Silverberg
Dr. Sidney & Eleanor Silverman
Jo Anne Simon

Dr. William & Barbara Skiba
Smart Interiors
    Murray & Dolores Smart
    Robert & Lauri Capozza
    Derek & Kim Backman
Dr. Ashok Soni
Iris Spano
Lilian Sperber
Dr. Harold & Jacqueline Sussman
Katherine Switzer
Gloria P. Tannenbaum
Dr. Dennis & Karen Tarnow
Harley Tomey
Drs. Francis & Nousha Tung
Dr. Bruce Valauri
Dr. Mary Jane (MJ) Vallee
Dr. Frank J. Vascimini
Michael & Olive Vassay
Dr. James Verna
Dr. William T. Waldinger
Dr. Stanley & Ellen Weinstock
Howard Weisberg
Dr. Arnold & Myra Weisgold
Dr. Lawrence & Lauren Weiss
Dr. Ronald S. Wilensky
Sam & Phyllis Wurtzel
Dr. Jonathan & Diane Zamzok
Justin & Dorothy Zizes

ACKNOWLEDGMENTS

In 1981, New York University College of Dentistry pioneered a progressive program that involved screening, identification, counseling, and support service for students with learning disabilities. Many individuals contributed to the success of the program. Dr. Charles Drake and Carolyn Olivier formulated the screening test that was essential in detecting first-year students at risk for learning disabilities. After the students were screened, Marty Patwell, Dr. Allen Parks, and Dr. Gloria Tannenbaum were instrumental in developing a definitive, in-depth psychoeducational diagnosis.

For many years, I have dedicated myself to help alleviate the problems faced by professional school students with learning disabilities. I have been assisted by many generous individuals. I am indebted to this community of dedicated persons. To them much is owed.

My profound gratitude to Dean Richard Mumma, Jr. of New York University College of Dentistry, for giving me the opportunity to initiate the learning disability program. My deep respect to his successor, Dean Edward Kaufman, who had the wisdom to see the advantages of the program and allowed the program to continue. My sincere thanks to Dr. Francis Panno, Jr., Chairperson of my Department, who allowed me precious time away from my dental teaching responsibilities to direct the program. I would like also to credit Dr. Carolyn Fuss who, as Director of Student Affairs at the College of Dentistry, helped secure the support so essential for the program's success.

My appreciation and heartfelt gratitude to Dr. Rosemary Bowler for so generously sharing her time and expertise. Her wizardry with the English language, her inspired suggestions, and her thoughtful responses improved this book and helped its author to transcend his limitations.

I am grateful to my friends Carolyn Olivier and Joyce Pickering for their untiring support.

Most important, I thank Ronald Cohen, a dear friend for more than thirty years, who helped in editing this text. I deeply appreciate his wisdom and judgement in helping organize the material. If errors or inaccuracies occur in the text, I bear sole responsibility.

Traditionally, authors acknowledge their wife for emotional support, patience, understanding, etc. My wife, Iris, is certainly due that, but also much more. She contributed in more ways than I can count. To whatever quality this book may possess, she was invaluable.

Finally, I recognize all those students who participated in the program and triumphed over their learning disabilities. Without their dedication, persistence, perseverance, and trust in me and the program this success story could never be told.

Stanley J. Antonoff

TABLE OF CONTENTS

PREFACE

The term **'learning disability'** is defined in The Americans With Disabilities Act of 1990 (PL. 101-336). It is a disorder in one or more of the basic processes involved in understanding spoken or written language. It may appear as a problem in an average intelligent individual's ability to think, listen, speak, read, write, spell, or do math. The term 'learning disabled' does not include individuals who have learning problems which are primarily the result of visual, hearing, or physical handicaps, mental retardation or emotional disturbance; nor does it include individuals with environmental, cultural, or economic disadvantages.

Until recently, dyslexia and related learning difficulties were a mystery to most parents, teachers, and professionals. Many believed that dyslexia was a problem related to vision. Another popular myth asserted that problems associated with learning disabilities disappear in adulthood. If this premise were true, a student could not have academic difficulties in graduate and professional school because of learning disabilities. However, students with learning disabilities are identified in graduate and professional school. In these cases, the student's treatment is usually based on the same educational strategies employed with secondary school or junior college students.

It has been estimated that 3 percent of all undergraduate students have learning disabilities. Nicholas Negroponte, the founding Director of the Media

Laboratory at the Massachusetts Institute of Technology (MIT), has noted that dyslexia is so common at MIT that it is locally called "the MIT disease." Many unidentified students have persevered over their disabilities and successfully completed graduate and professional schools. Other students with disabilities have not been successful. Students with learning disabilities can succeed best in both their academic and social environments if their learning difficulty is properly diagnosed at an early age and the appropriate remediation implemented.

To achieve academic success, students with learning disabilities often require a support system. Having the succor of parents, friends, and teachers is essential for the individual with learning disabilities. Support and understanding build a level of confidence in the student which helps maximize the development of needed compensatory mechanisms. We create our experiences by the way we operate our minds. If the student is optimistic, this creates a positive environment that is essential for surmounting his problem. However, it requires teamwork. Both the student and the educational advisor must work together aggressively to ensure that the problems associated with learning disabilities are ameliorated.

Before the start of the Learning Disability Program at New York University College of Dentistry, students with learning disabilities were not identified as such. Furthermore, learning disabilities were not considered a significant reason for failure at the graduate and professional school level. Implicit in this outlook was the belief that a student with learning disabilities could not successfully complete a college program, nor be accepted into a graduate or professional school. Before our program was instituted, students who failed and were suspected of having learning disabilities were subsequently tested. Usually, the testing occurred at the end of their freshman year. Unfortunately, by that time, they had either left dental school voluntarily or were asked to leave because of their failing academic record. Some students petitioned the administration to repeat the freshman year. In certain cases, they received permission to do so. The administration felt that repeating the year would give these students a further opportunity to grasp successfully the course material. Frequently, these students failed again because they did not know how to deal with their problem.

The program we initiated at New York University College of Dentistry was designed to help students with learning disabilities graduate from the dental school. The program was predicated on two basic principles: namely, caring for, and supporting these students. We hoped to eliminate or at the very least reduce student anxiety and fear of failure. This would also help to make the student's educational experience more meaningful.

The program was remarkably successful. Seventy-five percent of the students identified with learning disabilities graduated from the dental school. Many of these students have continued academically to achieve specialty status. Several are now teaching at the professional school level. The pro-active program at New

York University College of Dentistry was the first of its kind anywhere in the world. Usually, we identified students with learning disabilities in the sixth week of their freshman year and immediately instituted mechanisms to enhance their education and reduce the possibility of their failure.

At the beginning of the program, our core mission was to identify students with dyslexia and help them succeed. We soon discovered that the screening and subsequent in-depth psychoeducational testing also identified students with other types of disabilities. As our testing mechanism became more refined, we were able to identify students with Attention Deficit Disorder (ADD) and Attention Deficit Hyperactivity Disorder (ADHD). Approximately 20-25 percent of individuals with ADD or ADHD have a co-morbidity with dyslexia or other learning disabilities.

Today, the New York University College of Dentistry Learning Disability Program no longer exists. A new administration decided to rely on the assistance of the central learning disability support personnel of New York University. Unfortunately, these support personnel, who were well trained to assist students at the undergraduate level, had little understanding of the unique problems of students with learning disabilities in graduate and professional school.

I decided to write this book so that the concepts and foundations of the original program are not relegated to the dust heap of history. In this text, I have preserved the strategies used to help students with learning disabilities succeed and described the program's components. I have also included an appendix incorporating several important elements of the program: the screening protocol, the screening sub-tests, and the methods used for scoring. In this manner, a twenty-year accumulation of information will be available to future researchers for reference, for expansion, or for testing its validity.

PART I

⇒✦⇐

THE PROGRAM

⌣   ⌣

INTRODUCTION

The reason I have dedicated myself to help alleviate the problems faced by students with learning disabilities is personal. In 1962, my oldest son Steven, seven years old, was having great difficulty learning to read and to write in public school. As concerned parents, my wife and I took him to the New York University Testing and Advisement Center. He was given rigorous testing to determine his areas of deficiency, if any, and to develop a course of treatment that would help improve his school performance. After four days of testing, the diagnosis revealed that Steven had normal intelligence. However, he had many strengths and weaknesses in his capacity to learn. A high level of inconsistency was evident in his performance. This is termed "spiking." It indicates his strengths that are graphically shown above a median and his weaknesses, which fall below this median. The Center suggested that Steven could be helped by attending a military academy. My wife and I felt differently. We believed that a warm and nurturing family environment was more important. Therefore, Steven remained in public school where we could monitor his academic performance and immediately provide the needed support.

In light of our knowledge of dyslexia today, the Testing Center's conclusion was flawed. However, it must be viewed in perspective. The International Dyslexia

Association (IDA), then called The Orton Dyslexia Society (ODS), was less than fifteen years old. The information concerning the effects of dyslexia was understood only by a few individuals. Furthermore, the available knowledge concerning dyslexia and other learning disabilities was not predicated on any scientific foundation. The existence of learning disabilities was seriously debated. Many educators and scientists did not believe learning disabilities was a real entity. Federal and state funds for these students were unavailable because learning disabilities was not a definable, quantifiable entity supported by empirical evidence.

The first law that ensured the right to a free, public, appropriate education for students with dyslexia and other learning disabilities, Public Law 94-142 (re-authorized many times and today known as IDEA), was not passed until 1975. In 1962, students with learning disabilities were rarely diagnosed correctly. Few educators knew how to deal with the student or the problems associated with learning disabilities. No visible signs such as crutches, hearing aids, or glasses were evident, so learning disabilities became known as the "invisible handicap." Educators set low expectations for these students. Scientific knowledge about learning disabilities was minimal; subsequently, the education provided for these students was inappropriate.

Steven, a very poor reader, struggled through third and fourth grades. He had poor penmanship and inadequate writing skills. He did poorly on written tests; however, he knew the answers when questioned orally. In 1965, when our family moved to another city, Steven found himself in a more challenging public school system. He was in the fifth grade and at a greater disadvantage in this school setting. He continued to do poorly. Frustrated, we again took him to the New York University Testing and Advisement Center for in-depth psychoeducational testing. They confirmed the earlier diagnosis. However, with the military school placement, they also recommended Steven see a psychiatrist, since he was acting out and developing emotional problems. After several visits, the psychiatrist discharged Steven because he discovered no underlying cause for his incipient emotional problems. The psychiatrist suggested that his problems should disappear as he matured, a convenient solution to the problem. Today, we know that dyslexia does not disappear in adulthood. In fact, early identification and treatment will result in fewer problems persisting later in life.

Steven graduated from high school with average grades and was accepted at a Midwestern college where he matriculated with a less challenging curriculum. After one year, Steven left college because he was failing all courses. This occurred in 1974, one year before Public Law 94-142 was passed by Congress.

Steven, always a hard worker, returned home and found a good paying job. Encouraged by his family, he decided to attend a local, two-year Community College. This was a crucial step toward the college degree he always coveted. Beginning in 1975, Steven attended college at night, twelve months a year. After completing the two-year community college requirements, he was accepted into a four-year state college. Upon graduation, he was accepted into a Master's program and now holds a Master's degree in criminal justice.

Initially, Steven's problems were diagnosed as emotional in origin. Actually, the emotional problems were secondary to his learning disability. A missed diagnosis was based upon a lack of information about learning disabilities. Steven graduated from college without knowing he was learning disabled. His dyslexia was finally diagnosed in 1979.

THE DIAGNOSIS:

Steven's two younger brothers, Charles and Kenneth, had similar academic difficulties. By 1979, more educators and psychologists were knowledgeable about learning disabilities. Several professionals suggested that we take Charles and Kenneth to Massachusetts General Hospital in Boston for testing. After exhaustive testing, Dr. Perlo, Director of the Language Clinic, indicated that both boys were dyslexic.

We reviewed Steven's old test results and realized that he was also dyslexic. Steven had completed college without knowing of his learning disability. Today, irrefutable evidence reveals that many students complete college and graduate and professional schools without ever knowing they have dyslexia or some other learning disability. Their academic success is due to perseverence and an ability to develop compensatory mechanisms to overcome or bypass their disorder. One reason that some students fail academically is their inability to compensate for learning problems.

THE IDEA:

After Charles and Kenneth were diagnosed, we learned that our school district was not sufficiently knowledgeable in the techniques and strategies necessary to educate dyslexic children. We sent Charles and Kenneth to a private school specializing in teaching children with learning disabilities. Both Charles and Kenneth[1] went to Landmark School in Prides Crossing, Massachusetts.

This is where the journey begins. Dr. Charles Drake, the Headmaster at the Landmark School and I became good friends. One day at lunch 'Chad,' as he was

---

[1] Charles graduated from Landmark School, enlisted in the United States Coast Guard and was injured while on active duty. He is presently on 100% medical disability. Kenneth attended Landmark School for four years, followed by three years at prep school. He then went to Barbara Cordoni's learning disability program at Southern Illinois University and graduated in five years. He attended graduate school for one year to secure sufficient science credits to enable him to attend dental school. He was accepted into New York University College of Dentistry and graduated with a DDS degree in 1995. He now practices dentistry.

affectionately known, made a startling statement. "Stan, the medical profession, including dentistry, is flooded with dyslexics." My immediate response was one of skepticism. How could he make such a generalization without any corroborating evidence? "Just look at the scribble on their prescription pads. Their handwriting is terrible. This is one cardinal sign of dyslexia!" he exclaimed. He could not be convinced that the poor handwriting might be the result of the doctor's hectic schedule. Furthermore, I could not believe that he based his conclusion solely on this observation.

Chapter One

RATIONALE

I was quite perplexed and concerned. If 'Chad' Drake were correct, many students with learning disabilities could be found in graduate and professional schools. Was this a possible explanation why some students failed the academic program? Additional questions stimulated my interest. How did their learning disabilities affect their ability to deal with the curriculum? Could they still become good physicians, dentists, or professionals in other fields? How would this affect the school's reputation if the profession and the public learned that the institution graduated students with learning disabilities? Would these students be considered inferior to their peers and therefore be held in low esteem? The next questions were personal. Assuming students with learning disabilities attended dental school, how could we locate them? If found, did they need assistance? Could we help them through the rigorous academic program? These questions and others needed to be addressed.

STUDENT ISSUES:

To paraphrase the late doyenne of dyslexia, Margaret

Rawson, "dyslexia has many faces" and this aphorism applies to other learning disabilities. If we could develop a program to aid students with learning disabilities at the graduate and professional school level, its goal would be to help students overcome the disability and master the curriculum. If the forms of this disability share one common feature, it is that affected students work more slowly than their non-learning disabled counterparts. These students take longer to visualize, process, identify, and respond to a stimulus. At graduate and professional school, they often do not have time to master the course curriculum and undergo remediation concurrently.

As we considered the needs of our dental students, several of us decided to develop a program for them. Such a program would require identifying at-risk students and encouraging them to undergo a proper diagnosis. For those students diagnosed as dyslexic/learning disabled, we could then devise appropriate bypass and support mechanisms. Most of these students had succeeded at high school and college levels without knowing of their learning disability. We could refine and augment their existing compensatory mechanisms to help reduce their learning difficulties and provide the tools for success. Our goal was to encourage students with learning disabilities to cope with their learning problems. Coping is the positive approach and achievement is the result. Their prior successful compensatory mechanisms could be taken to another level to assist in achieving academic goals in dental school.

Many approaches for educational achievement for

these students at the graduate and professional school level are predicated on techniques originally used for children. Structure and multi-sensory learning strategies are of primary importance. Graduate and professional school students with learning disabilities should be instructed in the use of these special learning techniques to maximize academic achievement. At higher levels of education, finding sufficient time to eliminate weaknesses is difficult. Therefore, we must concentrate on using the student's strengths.

The institution of the extended five-year program at New York University College of Dentistry was very effective in helping these students succeed. The five-year program, discontinued in the 2000-2001 academic year, gave students with learning disabilities the necessary time to develop bypass mechanisms or refine those already being used. It is important that students with learning disabilities be knowledgeable about their personal strengths and weaknesses.

Several students prior to entering New York University College of Dentistry knew they were learning disabled, since they were identified earlier in their academic careers. However, few of these students had their particular strengths and weaknesses clearly explained to them. They had little or no understanding concerning the ramifications of their learning disability. They simply knew that a reading problem (decoding, comprehension, or memory) or an auditory problem existed. One student believed he could not hear well. A student needs more than a superficial awareness of his disability. He needs precise knowledge of his strengths and weaknesses. This information must also be made available to the teaching faculty it they are to help the student improve his academic performance. For example, a student with an auditory processing problem must understand that a series of spoken commands could be very difficult for him to process. In this situation, the strategy recommended is for the student to request the instructor to recite the commands slowly so he can write them down. Of course, there are real world consequences to such a request. Such requests may annoy the instructor. However, if the request is preceded by the courteous statement that the commands are crucial and the student does not wish to miss them, this should help eliminate any potential problem, as well as minimizing the student's stress.

Alexander Astin is the director of the Higher Education Research Institute at UCLA. Research from this Institute reveals that behaviors, attitudes, and levels of stress exhibited by students today are higher than those displayed by earlier generations. Stress can adversely affect the ability of students with learning problems to develop compensatory mechanisms, thereby affecting their ability to learn. Fully one-third of college students reported taking a basic skill or remedial course in reading, mathematics, or writing. This illustrates either an inadequate earlier education or the inability of these students to grasp presented material because of differing learning styles. Because of diverse learning styles, we need to create educational environments for students today that enhance learning and consequently academic success. Students with learning disabilities should be viewed as individuals with special needs, unique differences, and singular potential. It is most important that teachers demonstrate sincerity, caring, and a willingness to respect the complexity of each student.

Dwight Eisenhower, Supreme Commander of Allied Forces in Europe during World War II and later President of the United States, often said that plans are everything in a war but once the battle begins, plans are worthless. The same can be said about adult students with learning disabilities. The planning process before a battle is akin to the diagnosis of learning disabilities. Finite measures can be established for both. What cannot be predicted during battle is the enemy's reaction. For adult students with learning disabilities, the effect on learning of personal experiences and psychological make-up cannot be predicted. The diagnosis of learning disabilities in a young child allows for remediation with little interference from the psychological scars of anxiety, frustration, and failure. This luxury is not available with adult students. Therefore, their success is problematic and unpredictable.

My conversation with Dr. Drake was the next step in the journey. Could a test be devised that would support "Chad's" theory? I was certain that a significant number of "subjects" to test could be assembled. Dr. Charles Drake and Carolyn Olivier developed a battery of screening tests that measured various basic skills believed to reveal the presence of learning disabilities. (See page 24).

The development of a battery of screening tests that could assist in identifying students with learning disabilities before academic failure occurred would enhance their likelihood of success in dental school. Students with learning disabilities would be emancipated from the "second class" educational status they presently held.

The purpose of this text is to present the Learning Disability Program and to present guidance to help students with learning disabilities be successful at the graduate and professional school level.

Chapter Two

THE
JOURNEY _____

The beginning of emancipation for individuals with learning disabilities in the United States can be marked by the enactment, in 1975, of the Education for All Handicapped Children Act (US PL. 94-142). This and additional legislation, including Section 504 of the Rehabilitation Act of 1973 (US PL. 93-112) and more recently the Americans With Disabilities Act (US PL. 101-336), have contributed to the growth of programs for students with learning disabilities at the elementary and secondary school levels. In fact, the enactment of the Americans With Disabilities Act represented a historic landmark in the disabilities' equality movement. Upon signing this legislation, President George Bush described the Act as a "historic new Civil Rights Act . . . and the world's first comprehensive declaration of equality for people with disabilities." Among the factors shaping the educational landscape of the learning disabled is the progress through our educational system of students with learning disabilities. Many children identified since the passage of PL. 94-142 and IDEA have graduated from college and are attending graduate and professional schools. These laws have enabled more students with learning disabilities to receive support services, thereby maximizing their ability to succeed academically. Success at the secondary school level has encouraged students with learning disabilities to pursue further their education at colleges and universities. Their achievement has resulted in more students applying to and matriculating at graduate and professional schools ill prepared for their arrival. We became victims of our own success. The rising tide of students with learning disabilities in higher education places new demands and increasing pressure on colleges, universities, and especially on graduate and professional schools to respond to the needs of these students.

CLASSIFICATION

Students with learning disabilities who have matriculated through the educational process at the post-secondary level may be classified in two categories: those who know they are learning disabled and those who are unaware of their learning disability. Both groups often achieved academic success at the college level. However, at graduate and professional schools, success for both groups is much more problematic.

FAILURE FACTORS

There are several explanations for the poor academic performance of students with learning disabilities in graduate and professional school. The failure factors often cited are the same factors attributed to children with learning disabilities who do poorly: inadequate schooling; inadequate skills development; poor cognitive development; lack of motivation; work experiences; family aspirations; and cultural and ethnic development. Little information exists about the intellectual level and basic skills needed by adults with learning disabilities in order for them to succeed academically. As they grow older, some individuals with learning disabilities display fewer problems. This may be attributed partially to their mastery of segments of their learning problem. This mastery is often achieved by the constant repetition of tasks.

Until recently, the myth that problems associated with learning disabilities would disappear in adulthood was a common belief among professionals. Treatment was based on the same educational strategies employed with secondary school or junior college students. Today, we understand that in order to eliminate or significantly reduce the problems faced by adults with learning disabilities, we must identify the specific disability and the associated specific academic skill deficiency. Procedures for identifying adults with learning disabilities are often abused and frequently not helpful, perhaps because an adult with a learning disability does not show a highly visible disability. When such an adult participates in a post-secondary educational program, the learning disability may be undetected by the adult and the teachers.

Many post-secondary institutions have tried to level the playing field by establishing study skill centers, by hiring support personnel to work with disadvantaged students, or by sponsoring programs for students with learning disabilities. Some programs provide adjunct diagnostic services, but few offer class-wide screening to help determine whether a student is learning disabled. Post-secondary institutions may incorrectly assume that students with learning disabilities know their problem exists, and, therefore, will seek needed services. However, many students at academic institutions, especially at graduate and professional schools, are unaware of their learning problem; consequently, they do not seek needed services.

Students with learning disabilities who experience a high degree of academic success in undergraduate school are lulled into a false sense of intellectual security. As the student ascends the academic ladder, he may frequently encounter faculty members who are unaware of the existence of the problem entitled "learning disability," and who do not understand the basic needs of these students. Unfortunately, this lack of knowledge and understanding is prevalent among teachers in graduate and professional schools.

Chapter Three

THE
PROGRAM _____

To address the problem of students with learning disabilities doing poorly at the professional school level, New York University College of Dentistry pioneered a program that supported and counseled these students. In 1979 and 1980, the College of Dentistry researched the effects of learning disabilities on professional school students, specifically, how their particular learning disability slowed their capacity to learn in certain academic disciplines. As a result, we designed and implemented a support program for improving the performance of students with learning disabilities. The program's primary goal was to identify and provide the necessary tools for students with learning disabilities to succeed in dental school. To facilitate this goal, our first objective was educating the professors. We believed it critical that they understand that students with learning disabilities often have great potential and that these students should be provided with appropriate support necessary for academic success. Beyond basic support measures, the program had to be aggressive in finding ways to improve the learning efficiency of these students. About our instructors, the aphorism that education's purpose is to replace a closed mind with an open one was true. Initially, we had to teach the teachers. The new program was innovative in design and revolutionary in format. The program's researchers believed that a student with a learning disability, who had average or superior intelligence, would have sufficient time in undergraduate school to compensate for most learning deficits. However, once the student entered dental school, new factors often caused students to do poorly. These factors included an eight-hour school day, five school days a week, and many more necessary study hours. Additionally, there was a lack of time to compensate for inadequate basic skills associated with a learning disability. Furthermore, there was a need for these students to develop new, highly refined perceptual and kinesthetic skills.

The learning disability program involved screening of students to determine which students were "at risk." This was followed by in-depth psychoeducational testing and, depending upon the findings, the institution of appropriate support services for these students. The objectives of the program included:

1. To determine the student's strengths and weaknesses. This was accomplished through screening and in-depth psychoeducational testing.

2. To determine whether the student had a particular "learning style." Again, testing would be invaluable.

3. To help the student meet academic requirements, where necessary, through curriculum adjustments, improved test-taking and study techniques, and the development of compensatory mechanisms.

4.To help the student achieve a meaningful educational experience by teaching the student better methods for processing and retaining information. Additionally, we would try to help the student psychologically to build self-confidence.

5.To graduate a knowledgeable, competent dentist able to meet the rigorous demands of the dental profession.

6.To help make accurate comparisons with students without disabilities and

7.To meet legal requirements.

The most significant aspect of the learning disability program involved identification of those students "at risk" and the institution of support services before serious failure factors developed. The screening mechanism actively sought out each student having a learning problem on an interceptive, pro-active, and preventive basis. Further testing provided information about each student's strengths and weaknesses not derived from the initial screening process.

PROGRAM INGREDIENTS

Professional schools seeking ways to promote success among students with learning disabilities may find the NYUCD program a model they can adopt or adapt for their disciplines. The following components are necessary for a successful program

Director - A successful program for students with learning disabilities at the graduate and professional school level requires first, and foremost, a dedicated director. This person must have a fundamental knowledge of learning disabilities and also be sensitive to the needs of students who have this problem. The director must be knowledgeable about the laws concerning the learning disabled. He should be able to interpret reports from psychometrists and must have the capability to help students develop compensatory mechanisms. He must be committed to learning and understanding the psychological profile of each student with disabilities. The director plays a critical role in helping students alter attitudes and behavior likely to inhibit their success. He serves as an advocate, guiding these students through the rigors of the program. He fosters a nurturing system that supports the embattled self-esteem of the student with learning disabilities. These students, successful at the undergraduate college level, now are often at the brink of failure. They have suffered a severe shock to their ego structure. While academic problems are the primary concern of these students, they often experience other problems such as test anxiety, sleep disorders, and depression. For students at the graduate and professional school level, the diagnosis of learning disabilities is both enlightening and frightening.

The director also plays an adversarial role. Underlying this position is the obligation to educate and be pro-active with other members of the faculty, administration, and staff. The director literally fights for the rights of the student with learning disabilities. Although Section 504 of the Rehabilitation Act of 1972 and the Americans with Disabilities Act, passed in 1990, delineates the accommodations available to the learning disabled, the law is not clear and often is subject to court interpretation. In this area, the director can act effectively. A student who challenges the faculty or the administration is often in a no-win situation. However, the director (a faculty member), especially one who has established a reputation for academic excellence, integrity, and student commitment is more apt to achieve results for the student with learning disabilities and, indeed, for the program. The program director speaks the powerful message that discrimination against the learning disabled will not be tolerated.

Administration and faculty - A knowledgeable and supportive administration and faculty are extremely important to any successful learning disability program. (See Chapter Five, page 77).

A psychometrist - Another important element in a comprehensive learning disability program is a knowledgeable psychometrist who can accurately measure the strengths and weaknesses of each student and relate this information, pragmatically, to the program director. The psychometrist should make appropriate recommendations to help effect an improved student performance. The compatibility of the program director and the psychometrist is essential for a well-integrated program.

Students - The general student population must understand that offering extra time on examinations does not give an advantage to students with learning disabilities.

An understanding and supportive student body is crucial for a successful learning disability program.

SCREENING

Dental school admission officers have long recognized that student credentials that satisfy entry requirements are not necessarily accurate indicators of future student achievement. Though applicants are carefully screened using available data (undergraduate grades, interviews, Dental Admission Test (DAT) scores, and letters of recommendation), performance records in dental school show attrition, failure, and underachievement. A candidate's anticipated potential is often not reflected in actual performance. Journal articles and texts reveal that several possible causative factors may underlie poor performance in dental school, specifically: stress, non-discriminating selection procedures, and lack of student motivation.

It has been observed that the score on the reading comprehension component of the DAT may only be two or three (out of a maximum of nine) for candidates with otherwise acceptable entry credentials. Frequently, these same candidates may also have a Scholastic Aptitude Test (SAT) verbal score of 400 or less. Because dyslexia is a language problem, it can be predicted that students with learning disabilities would have depressed scores on both the reading comprehension component of the DAT and the SAT. This underachievement and low score production on standardized admission tests may indicate the presence of learning disabilities. Learning disabilities, a subtle factor often overlooked by admission officers and faculty, may occasionally be the primary cause of academic failure. The previously suspected causes of academic failure, (lack of motivation, stresses, etc.), may be secondary responses to the underlying learning disability.

A major premise of the NYUCD program was that a student with learning disabilities who had average or superior intelligence would have sufficient time in undergraduate school to compensate for his learning deficits and would be able to achieve a high grade point average. Therefore, if the student also obtained a reasonable score on the DAT, that student might be accepted to dental school.

Determining which dental students were learning disabled was the goal of our program. To determine the "at risk" status of first-year students, a battery of screening tests was administered. These tests measured various basic skills believed to indicate the presence of learning disabilities. The tests were designed to measure lower-level automatic, cognitive, academic skills known to correlate positively with school-related tasks among adolescents. The tests and basic skills measured are listed in figure 1. The actual screening tests used and the manner of their administration are presented in Appendix A. (See page 181). These screening tests helped identify several indicators found in students with learning disabilities. The screening tests assessed skills and abilities not measured by

Test	Measured Parameters
Berea Visual Motor Gestalt	Visual-perceptual motor functioning and short term visual memory.
Paragraph Copy/Handwriting	Speed & accuracy of copying a paragraph.
Oral Directions (Baker & Leland, 1967)	Auditory memory with a visual reference.
Coding (Wechsler, 1955)	Speed & efficiency in paper & pencil tasks: memorization of symbols.
Auditory Memory for Unrelated Words (Baker & Leland, 1967)	Non sequential auditory memory.
Spelling	Spelling words from phonetic representations.
Otis Lennon Mental Abilities (Otis & Lennon, 1969)	Speed & accuracy in performing standardized multiple-choice tests.
Listening Comprehension (Durrell, 1955)	Ability to encode a dictated story.
Arithmetic Coding	Memorization & manipulation of symbols.
Essay	Language organization, spelling, speed.

figure 1

the dental aptitude test scores, undergraduate grades, or course grades. Studies of DAT performance suggest low correlations between DATs, undergraduate grade point average, and the screening test. The DAT correlates with some dental school courses, but these correlations are low and account for very little of the variance in student performance. Results of the screening test support previous studies verifying that the DAT is not a good predictor of student performance in dental school. The screening tests embodied several concepts:

1. *Handwriting* - The original premise held that students with learning disabilities could be identified in graduate and professional schools through their poor handwriting. Speaking, listening, reading, and writing are language activities. Empirical evidence suggests that the human capacity for speaking and listening have a biological foundation. In contrast, writing systems are human inventions predicated on visual symbols to represent elements in spoken language. An individual who knows how to read and write has to understand what the symbols stand for in any particular writing system. Handwriting is one human activity by which we are often evaluated. Poor handwriting can be an important indicator of the possible presence of learning disabilities.

2. *Spelling* - Spelling is an extremely difficult task for most students because it involves several different visual and auditory systems. It is especially strenuous for the student with learning disabilities. Spelling problems may be the result of serial order memory problems, visual or auditory discrimination problems, gestalt problems, dialectical differences, or other problems. While the poor speller may never become exceptional, the individual can improve this skill. Continual practice can make the student an acceptable speller. This is another example of practice becoming habit and habit translating into skill.

The spelling sub-test consists of fifty words to be spelled in a prescribed amount of time. Phonetic representations of the words are given as a clue. For example, the word acoustics would be represented as a koo' sticks. Interestingly, it was not often the inability to spell that resulted in a student's low score but the difficulty in completing the spelling list in the prescribed time. A classical picture began to emerge on the spelling sub-test. Those words the student attempted to spell were often spelled correctly. The low score was due to lack of time and not necessarily due to the student's inability to spell the words.

Students with learning disabilities often have shorter verbal memory spans and difficulties with word retrieval. They "know" the word, but cannot retrieve it rapidly. They require more practice retaining new vocabulary items. In graduate programs, including medicine, dentistry, and other health professions, students find that each discipline has its own technical vocabulary. Misspelled words for the professional are not only an embarrassment but they can have dire consequences. It is imperative that medical prescriptions are legible. Otherwise, the patient could be given the wrong medication. Scribbling on a prescription pad is one way for the practitioner to disguise poor spelling. The writer assumes that the pharmacist can decipher the handwriting or will call the author of the illegible prescription for clarification.

3. *Processing Information* - The human brain is equipped to execute many different functions, including low-level, sensory-motor skills. In dealing with lower-level visual inputs, different individuals can process information at various levels of efficiency and speed. Often, this efficiency is related to the diversity of the stimuli presented. No better example of diversity exists than in the way individuals process information and the ways in which they learn. In a few cases, slowness in performance can be observed as one aspect of a generalized retarded or compulsive pattern in which the individual is slow at every task, no matter what its nature. Usually, however, the slowness is confined to specific functions that can be identified as tasks requiring automatization ability. Slow automatization ability is characteristic of many language disabled students. There is no "cure" for slow automatization, but developing coping mechanisms provides ways of compensating. Practicing a specific task is necessary in order for the student to reach peak efficiency on that particular skill. This is most important when studying. The student should review all information to the point at which he can recall it automatically.

Slow automatizers often have trouble retrieving information. This is further complicated by their inability to write quickly enough to finish timed examinations. Students with learning disabilities often require extra time on examinations. Slow automatizers may be severely penalized if they do not receive this additional time. Specifically in reading, the slow automatizer is at a particular disadvantage. Research reveals that different parts of the brain govern specific, relatively simple activities, such as distinguishing color or moving a finger. More complex activities and behaviors rely on interactions between these individual brain areas which unite to form functional "networks" similar to a computer network. There are large differences among people with reference to brain sectors and how these areas "network" to do complex actions. The use of multiple sensory channels allows information to be sent for processing by various parts of both hemispheres of the brain.

4. *Symbolic mental manipulation* - This is the ability to hold one item in mind while manipulating another. It is a very specific skill whose development varies among students. Deficiencies with symbolic mental manipulation may suggest the presence of learning disabilities.

5. *Memory* - This term is used to describe a multi-variable process. It is one of the most complex functions carried on in the central nervous system. There are at least three time-related functions in memory: 1) immediate recall, which occurs within a few seconds to a few minutes of seeing or hearing; 2) short term memory, which occurs within a few minutes to a few hours; and 3) long term memory, which lasts for a considerable time. Certain memory functions relate to motor learning, others to symbol learning, and others to relationships. Each kind of memory tends to function with separate and varying degrees of efficiency depending on the individual. The number of times a particular input must be seen or heard before it enters a functional recall state suggests the individual's learning efficiency. For example, certain individuals can grasp a particular bit of information almost immediately and repeat it as though it were learned, i.e., committed to long term memory in one day. However, the next day some of these individuals may have forgotten the information studied and also the presentation of the lesson. Others have difficulty with short term memory functions.

However, with time and repeated exposure, students may develop improved recall for specific bits of information. Additionally, their ability to relate pieces of information into a cognitive framework increases so that retrieving information becomes more rapid and efficient. Constant review and repeated exposure to information, coupled with associating it with information already in long term memory are vital to maximize learning efficiency. This involves not only repeating information but thinking about it in a meaningful way.

Visual memory for Symbols - Many students with learning disabilities lack the ability to remember graphic symbols. This may be related to immediate and short term memory. Constant repetition and bypass or compensatory strategies are necessary to improve this ability.

Auditory Memory - Auditory memory problems are unlike visual memory problems. Repeated attention can be focused on visual images, but auditory stimuli pass immediately. Students with auditory memory problems usually need to write down everything of importance. It is a survival strategy for success. Individuals with poor auditory memory need to be taught techniques for retrieving informational sources. Higher level cognitive approaches are often necessary to bypass this problem. The use of a tape recorder is frequently prescribed for preserving lectures or other oral information and this may be extremely helpful in the lower grades. However, it is not necessarily the solution at the graduate and professional school level. Information required to be learned in short time periods precludes the effective use of tape recorders.

6.*Gestalt Disorders* - Gestalt psychologists have searched for clues to understand how the human mind "knows." They suggest several steps in the process of seeing and hearing. First, we attend to the parts of a figure. Then we organize these parts into a whole figure or "gestalt" for final reception and understanding. The process, whether visual or auditory, is automatic in perceiving simple figures. Most adults do it unconsciously and rapidly. The skill used by the non-learning disabled adult to distinguish between a square and a triangle (by the number and angle of the corners, and the slope of the lines) is a learned behavior. Seeing a blind child make such a "visual" distinction very slowly (by using tactile sense and kinesthetics and counting the corners and sides of a wooden form) is analogous to what the sighted person with learning disabilities does with his eyes.

Many students are delayed in the development of their ability to observe and reproduce geometric forms or words. Most students, whether or not they are learning disabled, can reproduce a figure if they can see the figure in order to copy it. However, they may have difficulty or be unable to draw it from memory. Usually, the more severe the gestalt problem, the greater are the decoding disorders in reading. Words are composed of letters that are basically geometric forms. The difficulty or inability of the brain to deal with geometric forms affects to some extent the word recognition function in reading and this can lead to a reading disorder.

A gestalt disability usually expresses itself in deficient decoding skills, but it can be detected in other processes. The student whose drawings of what he sees in a microscope bears no relationship to what others are reporting may be suffering from a gestalt problem. In addition, a person with a learning disability may have a problem with figure recognition when part of the observed figure is incomplete. A student with this gestalt problem may have problems doing acceptable dentistry. For example, the student may be able to define the internal parts of the excavation of a tooth prepared to receive a filling, but not able to delineate its external requirements. There is no known "cure" for gestalt problems. The student must learn to cope. On a positive note, students can be taught bypass mechanisms that will offer some assistance. Having the student describe the figure verbally may help him to understand it, as will having him trace the figure either with a finger or with tracing paper. Some students find that making dots as targets for drawing lines helps to ameliorate the problem.

SCREENING PROTOCOL

After the appropriate sub-tests were assembled, we had to establish a protocol for screening. To do this, we consulted with the Dean who agreed with the research project's goal to ascertain whether students with learning disabilities were among the present student population. We received permission to test first-year students, but strictly on a volunteer basis. The most difficult problem was to find the time to screen these students whose schedules were very tight. Eventually, one hour was set aside after the student's lunch break. This time, coupled with their lunch hour, gave us the two hours needed for the screening test. Social security numbers were employed for identification of the test takers to protect the confidentiality of the possible "at risk" students.

The sub-tests were designed to screen for, rather than to diagnose, specific learning disabilities. We were reluctant to declare that our battery of tests indicated the presence of learning disabilities, but we believed a positive result suggested the likelihood of such a disability. It should be noted that the screening test was not designed to screen out students with psychological, emotional, or motivational problems.[2] The screening examination was designed to test a large number of students in one session. All visual parts of the screening test, such as the Berea Visual Motor Gestalt Test, were placed on slides for projected presentation. This allowed the screening of an

_____

2 Due to the linguistic nature of the tests, students whose native language was not English were expected to perform poorly because of a lack of proficiency in the language. This was confirmed statistically. Today, the number of English-as-a-Second-Language (ESL) students in dental school has increased. Some ESL students may have been learning disabled. We could not confirm this with in-depth psychoeducational testing because norms in their particular language were unavailable.

entire class at a single session.

The pilot study was conducted in 1979 with 75 first-year dental student volunteers. The test battery was administered in one two-hour group session. Results of the study revealed a distribution in five categories, ranging from conclusive absence of learning disabilities to the definitive need for further testing to positively identify those students that appeared to have learning disabilities. The results revealed the following:

1. Four students, or 5 percent of the sample, appeared to have learning disabilities. Though the results appeared to be quite conclusive, in-depth psychoeducational testing would be necessary for confirmation. All four students were doing very poorly academically.

2. Twelve students, or 16 percent of the sample, showed some indication of learning disabilities. This group could only be confirmed by further testing. Many in this group were doing poorly in dental school.

3. Six students, or 8 percent of the sample, had some problems but were compensating well. Their school performance was rated satisfactory.

4. Sixteen students, or 21 percent of the sample, showed problems that could be attributed to causes other than learning disabilities, such as English-as-a-Second Language.

5. Thirty-seven students, or 49 percent of the sample, showed no problems.

The results of the screening were shared with Dean

Mumma at New York University College of Dentistry who gave us permission to test all the students in the next entering class. Accordingly, in 1980, the same two-hour battery of tests, accompanied by a 30-item self-report history questionnaire, was administered during orientation week to 195 first-year dental students. This was the largest group ever tested. The group consisted of 152 males and 43 females. Prior to the screening, the criteria for psychometrically determining the "at risk" status of the sample were outlined. Each distribution of test scores was to be examined. Those students whose scores fell within the lower 10-15 percent of that distribution of test scores would be considered in the low group for that test. Students who fell within the low group on three or more tests would be deemed "at risk." All tests were scored by one doctoral-level educational psychologist experienced in administering, scoring, and interpreting such tests. Each test was scored for the entire group in random order. Apart from the background information contained in the self-report/history questionnaire, the scorer had no knowledge of the students' current academic performance in the dental program.

The grades of all first-year students were reviewed to determine whether they were experiencing academic difficulty during the first trimester of dental school. The students who did poorly on both the screening test and specific academic courses were interviewed to determine the factors contributing to their poor performance. Again, this represented approximately 5 percent of the sample. We recommended to the students that an in-depth evaluation at an independent assessment clinic would be helpful. For the first 1,000 freshman dental students screened from 1980 to 1986, the mean prevalence of learning disabilities was 5.5 percent.

Female students outperformed male students on a variety of tests, including writing tasks requiring acquisition and short-term retention or automatization of symbols. That the female students were significantly older than the male students may have contributed to their superior performance. In this sample, no specific reason for the later enrollment of females in dental school was ascertained.

Despite the reported skills on the self-report questionnaire, there was very little relationship between test performance and perceived strengths or difficulties in skill areas. There are several plausible explanations.

1. Since some students had experienced a high degree of academic success, they did not perceive any areas as particularly difficult.

2. Some students were inclined to report difficulties when all indicators were contrary to this self-perception.

3. The tests measured skills that are not directly perceived as relevant to academic success, although they may underlie skill acquisition.

Expecting first-year graduate or professional school students to perceive the relationship between inadequate decoding skills and comprehending written language is unrealistic; specifically, they are unlikely to know normative performance standards for basic skills and be able to relate their own performance to any perceived difficulties.

Based solely on the screening data, several issues evolved regarding intervention:

1. ESL students who scored low on these tests appeared to have different areas of weakness than non-ESL students who scored low.[3] The ESL students' problems, primarily auditory in nature, suggested a different focus of remediation, centering on understanding, comprehending and translating oral language. The low scores of the ESL students might include those students with learning disabilities that the screening sought to identify. They would require different remedial efforts.

2. Post analysis of students' grades might yield correlations between specific courses and specific skills.

---

3   ESL student's performance on the tests supported the contention that some of these students would do poorly. The ESL student had not developed sufficient basic language skills to do well. The most apparent area of weakness among the ESL group related to auditory tasks. The areas of difficulty reported by ESL students also appears to differ substantially from those reported by non-ESL students who did poorly on the tests. Students who reported skipping a grade in lower level schools performed significantly better than those who had progressed at the expected rate. These students may have had higher mental or cognitive abilities or may have been more advanced in perceptual-motor skills, which allowed them to skip a grade.

Students who have done poorly on the tests and in specific courses should be interviewed to determine possible reasons for their performance.

3. For those students scoring low on the test battery and identified as "at risk" for academic failure, a more extensive, in-depth psychoeducational evaluation is required to determine whether a learning disability exists. This will also provide information not available from the screening process.

An important outcome of this type of screening is the determination of concurrent validity. Screening per se can be a useful activity, but showing that the test battery is successful in identifying students with learning disabilities also identified by other clinical measures is necessary. The in-depth psychoeducational testing was conducted to determine whether the students were learning disabled and to establish the effectiveness of the screening. The testing corroborated that approximately 5 percent of the first-year class was learning disabled. The screening tests had a "hit rate" (the percentage of students on the "at risk" list given in-depth psychoeducational testing and subsequently found to be learning disabled) of more than 80 percent. The screening tests proved a powerful tool in identifying those failing students who were learning disabled.

Identification is the essential step in providing equal educational opportunities. First, the student must be properly identified as learning disabled. Second, the student should be taught study, test-taking, and other strategies necessary for success. With appropriate curriculum adjustments, the student will have the opportunity to use his talents and learn as effectively as his non-disabled peers.

THE DECISION

Based on these results we requested that Dean Mumma establish a permanent program to support students with learning disabilities at the College. Initially, he was reluctant, articulating several potential problems, namely, the faculty might not support such a program, public awareness that a significant number of students with learning disabilities were part of our student body could present a negative image of the dental college, and funds were presently unavailable to establish and maintain such a program.

Our argument for the program's necessity prevailed. Though the faculty had certain concerns, they were sensitive to our goal. Unfortunately, they had little knowledge about the learning requirements of students with learning disabilities. We believed if the faculty were appropriately educated about the learning problems these students faced, the concerns of most of the faculty could be diminished. Since the dental college was losing money annually, the cost of such a program was understandably of great concern. We advised the Dean that if the program were established, it would be self-supporting. In fact, financing to run the program was obtained from outside sources. When the program was finally instituted, a sizeable amount of money was raised from private sources and, not surprisingly, from the faculty.

At this time, I had been teaching for more than twenty years, and my faculty friends responded generously in financial contributions. With reference to the fiscal crisis at the dental school, we convinced the Dean that the program would be a financial asset. Unlike undergraduate colleges and universities, the transfer of students between different dental colleges is almost non-existent. Since the curriculum varies greatly among dental colleges, admission officers are extremely reluctant to accept transfer students.

If a student fails the dental program in the freshman year, tuition for the next three years is lost to the dental college. If the failure of one first-year student could be prevented, the tuition saved for the dental college would be substantial. At the time, tuition for dental school for each student was approximately $25,000 per year. If just one student with learning disabilities remained in dental school each year because of our intervention, eventually there would be six students in school paying annual tuition by the fourth year (one in the second year, two in the third year and three in the fourth year for a total of six). Thereafter, the dental school would receive a financial benefit of $150,000 each year, not counting any increase in tuition. Furthermore, students learn their profession by doing dental services for patients. The fees earned for these services by students with learning disabilities would produce additional revenue for the dental college.

The Dean agreed to establish the first support

program for students with learning disabilities in a professional school. A document was drafted by the Dean and approved by the College of Dentistry Executive Faculty Committee composed of all Departmental Chairpersons and Deans. It was an innovative and forceful declaration. It gave the Program full administrative support and incorporated the essential concepts of:

1. Extra time on examinations, both written and practical.

2. Alternative test formats and,

3. Other accommodations, such as testing in a quiet place and only one examination given in a single day.
It established the goals of:

1.Equal opportunity for students with learning disabilities.

2.Creating conditions to maximize learning.

3.Retention of students through curriculum adjustments and support measures.

The full text of this document appears in Appendix B. (see page 233).

In September 1981, following the presentation of the Dean's document, a memorandum from the Director of Student Affairs was sent to all Department Chairpersons and Course Directors. This was another important declaration. It stipulated the basis for the program and indicated the specific responsibilities of Department Chairpersons and Course Directors. It reaffirmed the essential concepts presented in the Dean's document such as the requirement for extra time for both written and practical examinations. Additionally, it indicated specifics about:

    1. Where examinations are to be given.

    2. Alternative testing formats.

    3. Tutorial assistance.

    4. Relying on the particular student to identify his best method of learning predicated on his particular problem. The full text of this memorandum appears in Appendix B. (see page 237).

SCORING

After the establishment of the Learning Disability Program, we found that employing a psychometrist to score all screening tests every year for an entire class would be a considerable expense. To reduce costs, we instructed a group of interested students in the methods of scoring the screening test. The work was divided so that two or three students would score a particular test, thus giving uniformity to the results. The students became quite proficient at the task. Our strategy was to recruit scorers from each freshman class. They would then be available for an additional three years. As the student scorers progressed to the second, third, and fourth years of dental school, we introduced new freshman to help. In this manner, the program always had a reservoir of students familiar with the scoring methodology. Each year we enlisted student scorers with a letter requesting their help. (See Appendix B, page 240).

After a few years, we instituted a simpler method of arriving at the list of "at risk" students. Instead of using the lowest scores on three tests, all test scores were added and a list was created consisting of composite scores for each student with the lowest scores being the student most "at risk." Through analysis of the data, we learned that the Berea Visual Motor Gestalt Test was the single best indicator of a student being "at risk." The five students with the lowest scores on this test, though their composite score might not have been low, were placed on the "at risk" list.

After all tests were tabulated, a sheet was prepared (see Appendix A, page 230) that contained the social security number of each student (names were never used) accompanied by his test scores. All scoring sheets, accompanied by the actual screening test from each individual, were sent to the psychologist for more definitive and final scoring. The essay and Berea sub-tests were scored by the psychologist, since these tests required greater expertise than the other tests. Finally, a list containing the composite score of all tests for all students, with the lowest scores at the top, was developed by the psychometrist. The lowest scores indicated those students at the greatest risk for failure. This final list also identified the five students with the lowest scores on the Berea Visual Motor Gestalt Test.

The Director of the program obtained from the Dean of Academics a list of all students doing poorly or failing the two most important courses in the first half of the freshman year, Anatomy and Biochemistry. The academic and screening lists were compared. Those students on the academic list who were doing poorly and also appeared at the top of the screening list because of their low composite score were deemed to be "at risk" of failing the dental school curriculum.

CONSULTATION

The Learning Disability Program Director invited the "at risk" students to attend an individual consultation session. At this meeting, the Director explained to the student the implications of his poor performance on the screening tests. He informed the student that doing poorly on the screening test did not necessarily indicate that he was dyslexic or had other learning disabilities. It was just one possible explanation for his poor academic performance. He told the student that an individual with a learning disability tends to work more slowly than one without such a disability. The Director explained that a learning disability does not imply "dumb." It simply takes longer for the student with learning disabilities to visualize, process, identify, and respond to information. To simplify the explanation for the student, we employed a computer analogy. Older computers could do what new computers can, but they did it more slowly. We strongly advised the student to take an in-depth psychoeducational battery of tests to determine whether he actually had dyslexia or other learning disabilities. If the in-depth testing showed that no learning disability existed, then we could explore other possible causes for poor academic performance, such as poor study habits or test-taking strategies, social or emotional problems, or an inappropriate career choice. We carefully explained to the "at risk" student that if a learning disability was discovered, the results would remain confidential between the tester and the student. Only at the student's request would the results be released to the Program Director. If deemed necessary by the student (after consultation with the Program Director), the Dean of Academics and others would be informed, but only on a need to know basis. At this point, we suggested that the student consider the implications of this information and discuss them with parent(s) or advisor(s).

At this consultation, some students readily reported previous histories of remedial reading instruction or supportive tutoring in language arts. This information was helpful in making the diagnosis of learning disabilities. Other students already diagnosed as learning disabled prior to their acceptance into dental school were occasionally "uncovered." They failed to disclose their disability for various reasons. Some felt it might hamper their acceptance into dental school. Others believed their undergraduate success indicated they could handle the rigorous dental curriculum.

We advised the previously unidentified student to contact the Program Director after deciding whether or not to take the in-depth psychoeducational testing. We described to students the advantages and disadvantages of being identified as learning disabled. Benefits to the student included:

1. Additional time on examinations.

2. Alternate methods of testing, when indicated.

3. Extended times to hand in required work, where possible.

4. Study and test-taking strategies training.

5. Be allowed to take the dental licensing examination with additional time and extended over a two-day period.

Disadvantages included:

1. The possibility that other students would become aware of the student's learning disability and treat the student in a negative manner.

2. The possibility that unenlightened faculty members might consider these students inferior.

We explained to these "at risk" students that the screening test was not intended to make a definitive diagnosis of a learning disability. Only the results of in-depth psychoeducational testing could corroborate such a diagnosis.

We told students that a positive diagnosis of dyslexia or other learning disabilities indicated the student might have difficulty completing the dental program. Learning disabilities would be a major factor in explaining the student's poor performance. The Program Director had many concerns. Was the student psychologically prepared to accept behavioral modification strategies to improve his ability to learn? Was the student willing to face additional hardships and undergo changes in his academic regimen to improve his chances of successfully completing the dental program? Finally, did the student understand he could be assisted?

Most students readily participated in the individual in-depth psychoeducational evaluations, but a few declined to do so. Some students, previously undiagnosed, approached the individual in-depth testing with an "I can't lose anything by doing this" attitude and hoped to discover possible causes for their difficulty in dental school. Others immediately went into denial, not willing to accept this possible diagnosis. These students convinced themselves that they could not have a learning disability, a "not me" attitude. They felt they were not working hard enough or not devoting sufficient time to the courses they had done poorly in or failed. Their solution was to spend more time studying the troubling courses and less time with their successful courses. This was termed "bargaining." This strategy usually resulted in continued poor or failing work because of a lack of necessary compensatory skills. After continuously struggling, many of these students returned for in-depth psychoeducational testing. In many cases, it was too late to help them; they had to repeat the first year.

At the consultation, many students with a previous diagnosis of learning disabilities or a history of remedial assistance reported that they coped with college workloads. However, they revealed having a great difficulty keeping pace with the increased workload/schedule demands of the dental college.

Over the years, successful students with learning disabilities did what was necessary to succeed and achieve their goals. The more they controlled their learning disability and created a positive and productive experience, the greater their success. Clearly, they had a strong desire to prove they could succeed. These students set goals, no matter how small, made moderate, incremental but significant advances until they succeeded. They did not have the attitude, "why me?" They expended energy finding ways to achieve. They recognized their disability as a disadvantage and hindrance and spent time accepting, understanding, and discovering ways to work around their problem. They arrived at their own way of doing things. With the assistance of the Program Director, they developed strategies that enhanced their ability to perform. They were able to recognize and take advantage of assistance from mentors and other supportive and helpful individuals and groups.

STUDENT INTERVIEW

An important aspect of the program was the student interview. In the interview, we looked at certain traits necessary for the student to be academically successful. Predicting success is impossible; however, a person's achievement is only limited by potential and by the ability to compensate for deficits. Students arrive at a learning style predicated on developing compensatory mechanisms. These mechanisms, coupled with potential, lead finally to achievement. Additional ingredients for success are motivation and perseverence. Students with learning disabilities can succeed in a favorable environment and with appropriate support. Early intervention is a crucial ingredient. A careful and complete evaluation of each student is the necessary groundwork for success.

Potential - We are all born with a certain fixed quantum of potential. Potential cannot be increased. It can be used fully, partially, or not at all. We often hear of a student working beyond his potential, achieving beyond expectation: one can achieve beyond expectation only because the student's potential exceeds expectation. Measuring potential is very difficult. Occasionally, some sense of potential can be ascertained from the in-depth psychoeducational testing. However, students with learning disabilities often test so poorly that potential is difficult to measure. In addition, our measurements of potential on the psychoeducational testing and in personal interviews are fallible. Tests or psychological profiles cannot always determine an individual's potential.

The teacher should be alert for the quiet, shy, poor testing student with great unfulfilled potential. That student is easily misplaced in the rapid pace of modern education. Educators must not allow learning disabled students with potential to be lost or pushed aside to accommodate non-learning disabled peers. Nor should these students with learning disabilities be neglected because the faculty cannot spend sufficient time to teach them. Educators must help all students achieve their potential.

Motivation - There are many problems associated with motivating students. Self-motivated students are often able to compensate for deficient skills. Others with an inner drive simply require help developing compensatory skills to reach their potential. Students lacking this inner drive require support if they are to develop the motivation necessary to achieve academic success. Motivating sources are either within the student or in response to some outside stimulation. Parents often employ such motivating strategies as begging, bribing, cajoling, and, on occasion, threatening. Results vary; some strategies fail, others succeed, still others have mixed results. One child is motivated and another is not. Different strategies work for different children. But without motivation, students are unlikely to reach their potential, especially at the graduate and professional school level, or to develop sufficient compensatory mechanisms for success. Students with learning disabilities will succeed if they understand their strengths and weaknesses and the way they learn most effectively. Participation in the learning program and a desire to succeed are significant steps toward success.

Compensation - Compensatory mechanisms are counterbalances or countering strategies developed to overcome or diminish skill weakness. Students with learning disabilities who ascend the academic ladder experience increasing difficulty with learning. Often, they underachieve and fail. Potential is a fixed entity and motivation is a particular state of mind. Compensatory skills can be learned. This area can make a substantial difference in student performance. Students with learning disabilities often cannot develop compensatory mechanisms on their own. Some lack the ability to refine previously established compensatory skills to meet increased educational demands. Compensatory skills can be taught. Learning compensatory skills is more difficult for students if their potential is not high. Furthermore, learning compensatory skills is also difficult for a student who lacks motivation. Obviously, learning compensatory skills will be virtually impossible if the student lacks both motivation and potential.

Perseverance - Perseverence, a persistence and determination in an undertaking, often makes the difference between failure and success. It is an essential ingredient for achievement. The acquisition of language and the refinement of our skills demand perseverence. Students with learning disabilities who persevere regardless of how difficult or frustrating the academic road have a strong chance of succeeding.

Potential, compensatory skills, motivation, and perseverence should be identified during the student interview and used to determine the strategies most likely to help the student through the academic rigors of graduate and professional school.

During the student interview at New York

University College of Dentistry, we searched for evidence of student skills or traits vital for academic success. We pointed out to the student those clues testing indicated as influencing his academic performance. If auditory processing was the area of weakness, he would find taking notes or processing information from lectures difficult. A reading deficit might prevent the student from effectively or quickly securing all the necessary information or from understanding and retaining the information after the first reading. Students whose decoding skills were slow and/or inaccurate often compensated by relying more on context or on guessing strategies. These strategies are of limited value as the predictability of the text decreases. As the difficulty with reading a paragraph increases and/or the number of words reducing context decreases, the ability of the student with learning disabilities to rely on context or guessing to determine meaning is hampered. Students whose decoding ability was intact might encounter problems with comprehension or with fixing information in long-term memory. Students need to know their specific learning disability and how it affects their ability to learn.

Armed with this information some students, especially those highly motivated and willing to persevere, decided they could compensate for their deficits and meet the challenges of the curriculum. They had implemented personal strategies and accommodations to support their learning styles. Such students could often go forward without any assistance from the program, but their progress was monitored by the program director and other faculty.

Students who began to fail were often too embarrassed to seek the support of the program director. One of the goals of the program was to monitor all identified students through their entire academic career. By following the performance of these students, the program director was able to offer advice and assistance if any student began to do poorly.

Students with minimal self-motivation and great anxiety might not have the confidence to continue on their own. They often sought support from the learning disability program. These students were informed there are no guarantees. Success is predicated on working harder and "smarter."

Ego support was another feature of our program. Students were reminded that they had the ability to learn, but they had a problem: a learning dysfunction that was interfering with their ability to absorb and integrate information which made it difficult for them to achieve academically. When students understood this, they often were able to make modifications in their academic regimen and adjustments in their study habits and test-taking techniques. Believing that reassurance is important to student's success, we emphasized that no one could make them feel inferior without their consent. The program director shared with these students examples of those with similar learning disabilities who had graduated from the dental school. In order to succeed, these students must believe they can and must be willing to make sacrifices.

Of course, not all students with learning disabilities

successfully completed the dental school curriculum. We stressed voluntary program participation which often was immeasurably helpful to the student. Taking part in the program, however, was not a guarantee for success. The possibility of failure existed no matter how diligently the student worked. For instance, one student identified as learning disabled in college worked diligently, but was unwilling to make any behavioral changes in his study and test-taking strategies. He expected his previous compensatory skills to be sufficient for success in dental school. Unfortunately, he rested a career on this premise and failed the freshman year.

In dental school, the difficulty in the first year centers on time and time management. Eighteen separate and distinct courses that begin and end at different times fills the first-year academic calendar. Anatomy and Biochemistry, which are heavily weighted courses, begin in September and do not end until the spring of the following year. A course such as dental ethics, which is not a high credit course, may start in September and last only for six weeks. Other courses may begin in November or December. Because of the varying curriculum, students, especially those with learning disabilities, have a great deal of difficulty managing time.

Only a few actual dental courses are given in the first year. Many heavily weighted dental courses make the second year much more difficult. Dental courses involve the use of the hands and require a great deal of time after school to complete assignments. Reading notes or studying an academic course while doing dentistry with your hands is impossible.

Some students are burdened with difficult outside distractions which become obstacles for success. Dedication to the goal of becoming a dentist must be paramount. One student who successfully completed the first year was married and had a child. In the second year, with its more difficult classes and assignments as well as the demands of marriage, he was left with insufficient time to study and began to fail. In this case, the program director was unable to achieve a change in his behavior, and the student, who had not prioritized his time, failed the second year.

During discussions with the program director, students were reminded that not every non-learning disabled student graduates from dental school. Logically, why should it be expected that every student with a learning problem graduate. Failure is a possibility; however, it is not the proverbial "end of the world." The student is still special; he is among an elite group accepted into a professional school.

During discussions with an at-risk student, we studied him carefully, especially his facial expressions. Did the student have a distant look on his face? This might suggest he was not listening or he was overwhelmed. He might be listening but not processing the information or he might not understand the importance of the problem. Student reaction to the discussion frequently appeared in the form of tension, anxiety, or fear. These offered clues to how the student might apply himself to the program. Did the student ask questions and did the questions display some inquisitiveness? Was the student sincere and willing to effect a change in behavior? Did the student grasp the problem and understand the difficulties of overcoming his particular learning disadvantage?

Sometimes, the in-depth psychoeducational testing suggested that the deficits were profound and the potential for success was limited. Emotional problems, severe anxiety, or stress can affect student performance by interfering with the ability to concentrate. Insecurity and reduced self-esteem are factors that further contribute to the difficulty or inability to learn. In one instance, the diagnosis revealed that the learning disability was caused by a severe emotional problem. On advice of the Program Director, this student left dental school and entered psychiatric therapy. When deficits were severe, the Program Director informed the student that it was questionable whether the student could complete the curriculum and graduate. In these cases, the student was presented with two options. The first was withdrawal from the dental school. This withdrawal should be before any course failures so the withdrawal would not affect the student's future academic choices. If the student continued and failed, then this failure would be on his permanent record. The second option required application for medical leave. Usually this was granted based on the diagnosis of a learning disability. A medical leave assumed the student would pursue appropriate treatment. Subsequently, the student would be readmitted to the dental school when the person or institution involved with the remediation certified that he had completed remediation and was now better able to master the dental school curriculum.

In the program's twenty years, four students applied for and received medical leave. One student did not seek remediation nor apply for readmission. Two students applied for medical leave, received remediation, and were readmitted. After remediation, both students retook the entire first-year. In essence, it took them five years to complete the dental school curriculum and graduate. Today, these two students are practicing dentists. One is presently on the faculty at New York University College of Dentistry and has contributed substantially to the success of his department. The other student is a recognized dental specialist. The fourth student applied for medical leave, received remediation, and was readmitted. This student subsequently failed and was dropped from the dental school. In essence, predicting which students will succeed is impossible.

The flow chart (figure 3) summarizes graphically the Learning Disabilities Program at New York University College of Dentistry. Graduate and professional schools should consider the steps in our program as a guide in developing programs for students with learning disabilities. The entire entering first-year class was screened for learning disabilities during orientation week. The screening tests were scored and evaluated and an "at risk" list developed. The student's grades in Anatomy and

Biochemistry were compared with the "at risk" list. Low or failing grades and an "at risk" listing indicated further evaluation. Students who appeared on the "at risk" list and

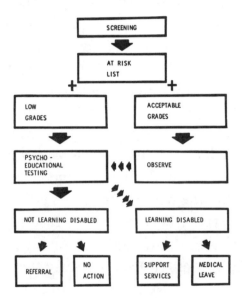

figure 3

had acceptable grades were closely observed. As they become overwhelmed by the pressure of trying to learn so much information, some may begin to do poorly or fail. Since such students may have a learning disability, we recommended that they undergo further psychoeducational evaluation. When no learning disabilities were found, either no action was taken or the student was referred to other resources. When specific action was not warranted, we still tried to help the student by personal attention outside the program.

If testing indicated a student had learning disabilities, we analyzed the test results to determine whether support services and curriculum adjustments would be sufficient for student success. If the disability would seriously impair the student's ability to matriculate, we recommended a medical leave. If the administration granted a medical leave, we recommended that the student pursue intensive remediation. If the remediation was successful, the student could return to school.

After the initial discussion with the director, the student had to decide whether to take part in the supportive program. We identified several reasons for students refusing this option. Some did not wish peers to know of their disability. Others refused because they already knew their strengths and weaknesses and felt they could compensate for their deficits. These students were offered personal support outside the official scope of the program. However, they could not receive official help such as extra time on school examinations and licensing examinations or taking examinations in a quiet place.

For those that sought official support, the program followed certain procedures. In the first instance, the administration and all departmental chairpersons on a need-to-know basis were given the names of those students diagnosed as learning disabled, along with a reminder of the support services available for these students. (See Appendix B, page 241).

Additionally, we sent a letter to each diagnosed student indicating that the administration and the departmental chairpersons had been notified of the student's learning problem. This letter further explained the student's responsibility for arranging for extra time on examinations and for securing any other available accommodations. Students at the graduate and professional school level must take charge of their own future. Though aided by the program director, they must learn to advocate for their own rights. However, they are admonished never to take an adversarial or argumentative posture with a faculty member. This is a no-win situation. In these instances, it was recommended that students defer to the program director who will advocate for them. (See Appendix B, page 243).

We reminded students that one of the reasons for poor course performance in professional schools is inappropriate application of time. The anxiety of the student with learning disabilities is another factor that must be considered in his studying and test taking problems. We informed him he might be suffering from secondary emotional problems resulting from feelings of frustration and inadequacy. These feelings might arise because of his inability to process and integrate information as rapidly as his peers. Frequently, we recommended psychological support. Test anxiety reduction and relaxation techniques are helpful in maximizing performance. Occasionally, students were referred to the school psychologist for stress and anxiety reduction techniques and anger management. We must go that extra distance to ensure the best results.

Because of the nature of dentistry, with its strong visual and depth-perception components, many of these students were being transformed from auditory learners (undergraduate school) to visual learners (dental school). It would take longer for them to develop appropriate learning styles, especially if they have a visual perception problem or poor short term visual memory.

The goals of the in-depth psychoeducational evaluation included identification of the specific disability, determining the student's strengths and weaknesses, and developing a list of recommendations for his improvement. They are usually standard recommendations determined by the results of the testing.

When we determine how the student best assimilates and processes information, we can provide strategies for success. There are three main learning styles: visual, auditory, and kinesthetic. Students may use all three, but one learning style usually predominates. Visual learners are most productive when relating to written information, diagrams, and pictures. Auditory learners find relating to information received aurally most efficient. Kinesthetic or tactile learners learn best through touch and movement, learning skills mainly by imitation and practice. While some students need only visual, auditory, or tactile input, others may require a combination of all three. This is known as multi-sensory learning. The student must know his strongest learning mode. A student who is a visual or an auditory learner needs to use that processing mode more frequently. Some students learn best when they use both visual and auditory processing simultaneously. Students who incorporate both into their learning style become proficient. Another theory of learning styles divides the brain into sides, where the left side of the brain is associated with language and is analytical and the right side of the brain is spatial and creative.

Other learning styles can be classified psychologically. Some students have learning styles that involve concrete perception, while others have learning styles that involve active and reflective processing. Students who learn through concrete perception absorb information directly through doing, acting, and feeling experiences. Active processors use the new information immediately, while reflective processors contemplate and think about new information as it is received. Student learning can be maximized and increased success occurs when information is presented in a student's particular learning style.

The program director and the student reviewed the psychoeducational testing recommendations. During the review, the program director reinforced the need to follow these recommendations. As an advocate, the program director helped promote the student's self-esteem by demonstrating interest and concern. The student was treated as a unique and worthwhile individual. This was accomplished by providing a warm, supportive climate, emphasizing each successful student accomplishment. It is easier to build a student's confidence than to repair a fractured one.

Chapter Four

OUTCOMES _____

Graduate and professional school faculties have been concerned about the ability of students with learning disabilities to complete successfully academic requirements. In 1997, the Learning Disability Program at New York University College of Dentistry undertook a study to measure some outcomes associated with student participation in our program.

METHODS

From 1980 to 1995, seventy-six students were identified as learning disabled and fifty-seven of those, or 75 percent, successfully completed the dental school requirements and obtained a DDS degree. In 1997, we surveyed by mail those students in the Learning Disability Program who had successfully completed the DDS program. The addresses of seven students with learning disabilities were not on record, so only fifty surveys were mailed. Also, we did not survey students who did not successfully complete the dental school curriculum. Twenty-six surveys were returned, a response rate of 52 percent. In addition, we sent surveys to 207 non-learning disabled graduates of the DDS program selected at random over the same fifteen-year period. Fifty-seven surveys were returned for a response rate of 27 percent. The total response rate was 32 percent. While it would have been statistically better if we could have surveyed the unsuccessful students with learning disabilities, the information derived from the survey was still valuable.

STUDY INSTRUMENT

We developed and mailed a 40-item self-report, survey form which contained, for the most part, forced-choice responses in the following areas: identification of learning problems, NYUCD learning experience, nature of learning disabilities, NYUCD learning disabilities program, overall appraisal, licensing exam, continuing education, residency, present activities, and personal information. Sections for comments from respondents were provided. Tables one through nine list the questions and responses received from the learning disabled and non-learning disabled groups. Too few responses were received to do a statistical analysis.

The survey indicates that the majority of the respondents with learning disabilities, (80.8%), were not so identified until they became students in dental school. An equally large percentage, (80%), of the respondents with learning disabilities believed that early identification helped them to be academically successful in their first year of dental school. A large percentage of respondents with learning disabilities, (88.5%), also indicated that "earlier" identification, before their entrance into dental school, would have made a difference in the quality of their educational experience, but would not necessarily have made a difference in their career choice. (See Appendix C, Table 1, page 251).

Thirty-two percent of the respondents with learning disabilities had problems learning and this translated into academic problems related to their learning disability for 27 percent of them. Some respondents with learning disabilities, (9.7%), had general problems learning not specific to their particular learning disability. A significant number of respondents with learning disabilities, (11.3%), did not want others to know they were learning disabled. (See Appendix C, Table 2, page 252).

Most respondents with learning disabilities, (42.3%), reported that their learning problems were both auditory and visual in nature. The results show a slightly higher percentage of visual, (30.8%), than auditory, (26.9%), problems. A majority of all respondents with learning disabilities reported that lecture courses were the most difficult, followed by laboratory and clinic courses. More respondents with learning disabilities, (75.9%), reported difficulty with lecture courses than respondents without learning disabilities, (60.7%). A smaller percentage of respondents with learning disabilities, (6.9%), reported difficulty with clinics, than respondents without learning disabilities (17.9%). (See Appendix C, Table 3, page 252).

Of all respondents with learning disabilities, 84.6 percent indicated that they participated in the Learning

Disability Program. Students with learning disabilities reported using a wide range of services offered in the program including additional time on examinations and study and test-taking strategies training. They found the wide range of program features helpful. Extra time on exams was rated the most beneficial program component, and support from fellow students was rated the least beneficial program component.

Most respondents with learning disabilities reported that direct assistance and support was most frequently received from the Director of the Program. (See Appendix C, Table 4, page 253).

Significantly, 90.2 percent of all respondents indicated that they were very happy or somewhat happy with their choice of a dental career. Virtually no difference in this question response was found between the two groups. Both the learning disabled group and the non-learning disabled group felt successful or somewhat successful (89.6%). However, the respondents with learning disabilities felt slightly more successful than the respondents without learning disabilities. Eighty-eight and a half percent of the respondents with learning disabilities felt that their learning disability had not hindered their performance in dentistry. Some respondents with learning disabilities, (23.1%), reported that their learning disability may have helped their performance in dentistry. (See Appendix C, Table 5, page 254).

A majority of respondents with learning disabilities, (52%), indicated that they received extra time while taking the written part of the licensing exam. Eighty-five percent of these respondents believed that it was beneficial.

There were considerable differences in the number of times each group needed to pass the licensing exam. Seventy-two and one half percent of the respondents without learning disabilities passed the licensing exam on the first time. But only 51.9 percent of the respondents with learning disabilities passed the first time. Only one respondent with learning disabilities had taken the exam and not passed compared with three respondents without learning disabilities who had not passed.

The most difficult part of the licensing exam was reversed for both groups. Almost 77 percent of the respondents with learning disabilities indicated that the written portion was the most difficult. However, 44.8 percent of the respondents without learning disabilities indicated that the practical portion was the more difficult. (See Appendix C, Table 6, page 255).

Most respondents with learning disabilities, 88.5 percent, felt that their learning disability did not interfere with their continuing education. (See Appendix C, Table 7, page 256).

Half the respondents with learning disabilities participated in a hospital residency after graduation compared to 62 percent of the respondents without learning disabilities. If sufficient residencies were available, respondents without learning disabilities were more likely to accept these opportunities (52.6% vs. 42.9%). A larger percentage of respondents with learning disabilities reported that they worked for an established dentist after receiving their license, (92%), compared to a smaller percentage of the respondents without learning disabilities (69.6%). (See Appendix C, Table 8, page 257).

There appears to be minimal differences in the current work arrangements between respondents with and without learning disabilities, with 36 percent for both groups reporting work in solo practice. A higher percentage of respondents without learning disabilities, 46.2 percent, became dental school faculty members upon graduation compared to 26.9 percent of the learning disabled respondents. A larger percentage of respondents without learning disabilities, 29.4 percent, held a hospital affiliation compared to 19.2 percent for the learning disabled respondents.(See Appendix C, Table 9, page 257).

DISCUSSION -

There is an increasing interest in the effectiveness of clinical interventions, services, or entire programs in health care settings. Measuring program satisfaction and examining clinical outcomes can determine their effectiveness. Outcomes can be conceptualized along three dimensions: clinical outcomes, utilization outcomes, and the measurement of satisfaction. Satisfaction surveys can provide direct reporting from participants (respondents) of attitudes, opinions, and views of the effectiveness of a particular program or service. During periods of scarce resources, competing demand for resources, and demand for justification of resource utilization, more attention has been directed toward demonstrations of positive outcomes.

The use of clinical outcomes has at least three important implications. They involve assessment of the person seeking treatment, emphasize change over time, and if change occurs, it should be attributable to the intervention itself.

Utilization outcomes can take the form of within-episode service use, concurrent service use, or end-of-treatment-episode level of care. For students with learning disabilities, within-episode service use involves the type and amount of services employed while in dental school as part of the learning disability program. Concurrent service use involves those services employed outside the learning disability program. End-of-treatment-episode level of care represents the services used or continued after dental school.

Surveys of satisfaction attempt to answer several questions, specifically, do people who use learning disability programs receive what they want, when they want it, and are the services of the quality that they expect? Consumer satisfaction, according to Lyons and his colleagues, has a number of dimensions as indicated in Table 10.

In terms of the various dimensions of satisfaction as described previously, several areas were addressed in the survey. Most respondents reported positively on the technical quality of the program. In fact, it had made a difference in their educational experience. They responded differently in terms of the program components. They reported that additional time on examinations, test-taking, and study skills development were the most helpful.

TABLE 10: DIMENSIONS OF SATISFACTION*

Dimensions	Definition
Technical quality	consumers' perception of the expertise of a service
Competence	the skills, level of training, and fund of knowledge of the person providing a service
Interpersonal Quality	the people encountered in the process of providing care
Access	the ease with which consumers can obtain desired services
Availability	whether there is option among a set of desirable choice of services and available services
Benefit/Value	Benefit = whether the individual perceives that he or she has gained something from participation in the service
	Value = combination of costs and perceived clinical outcomes

* adapted from the Rand Corporation, Ware & Hays, 1988 & Lyon, 1977

Uniformly, the respondents with learning disabilities found the Director of the Learning Disabilities Program to be most supportive in contrast to the support provided by other faculty members. The fact that the Program Director advocated for the interests of individual students with learning disabilities could explain this result. The survey indicated that after receiving their license, respondents with learning disabilities were more likely to work for established dentists than respondents without learning disabilities. This result may be attributable to a sense of insecurity many students with leaning disabilities have even after completing dental school. Employment by an established dentist would give respondents with learning disabilities the additional advantage of continued support. Additionally, it would allow time for further development of their dental abilities.

It appears that respondents with learning disabilities had a more difficult time with the licensing examination. Respondents with learning disabilities reported difficulty with the written part of the licensing exam. This result could have been anticipated, since the learning difficulty most frequently encountered was dyslexia, a language problem. This would explain the reason for the written part of the licensing examination being more difficult for students with learning disabilities.

It is apparent that the learning disabled respondents did not perceive much difficulty with the practical portion of the licensing examination. Two important aspects of the academic dental curriculum as well as the dental licensing examination are spatial sense and artistic inclination. This is reflected in the ability to do chairside dentistry. Both spatial sense and artistic inclination appear to be specially developed in dyslexics. Because of this, dyslexics appear to have characteristics specially suited for dentistry and the practical (non-written) portion of the licensing examination. In contrast, respondents without learning disabilities had difficulty with the practical (non-written) section of the licensing exam. Perhaps individuals without learning disabilities do not have as well developed spatial sense and artistic inclination as their learning disabled peers.

It is not clear why the respondents with learning disabilities were less likely to have participated in a hospital residency. Usually, obtaining a hospital affiliation is difficult if one has never served as a resident in a hospital.

The results also reveal that most students with learning disabilities felt that participation in the learning disability program gave them benefits that helped ensure their academic success. Overall, respondents felt positive about their dental career choice and, interestingly, slightly more respondents with learning disabilities felt that they were successful in their career than their non-learning disabled peers.

CONCLUSIONS -

This survey showed that satisfaction as a measure of outcomes could be assessed along several dimensions and that dental students with learning disabilities could be successful if they participated in a special program. It is evident from the results of the survey that students appreciated the learning disability program experience, specifically, the support from the program's leadership and the various program components. In fact, most of the students with learning disabilities reported a sense of success, and to some extent, their learning disability has made them more successful in dentistry. The respondents with learning disabilities clearly indicated that the Learning Disability Program provided accommodations that helped them complete their studies and helped them enter the profession of dentistry.

Many survey respondents reported that one of the most important results from their participation in the New York University College of Dentistry Learning Disabilities Program was the emotional support and resultant emotional well-being, improved self-esteem, and sense of success they received.

PART II

⇒✕⇐

THE INSTITUTION

⌣   ⌣

Chapter Five

FACULTY
AND
ADMINISTRATORS_____

In 1981, very few programs existed in the United States for students with learning disabilities at the post-secondary school level. Only one program existed at the graduate and professional school level, the program at New York University College of Dentistry.

Institutional commitment is necessary to sustain a successful program. The administration, faculty, and staff must be educated about students' needs including the appropriate accommodations. Further, it must be clarified to all that these are qualified students who can and will be an asset to their profession. By treating the student with learning disabilities in a professional manner, the administration will help remove any stigma associated with learning disabilities that may be perceived by unenlightened faculty members.

The key to a successful program is the faculty. If the faculty is uninformed, myopic, and believes these students are an undesirable burden on the system, the program will fail. The faculty must understand that students with learning disabilities learn differently; however, they are often above average. These students can add immeasurably to the overall value and diversity of the school program. By combining faculty, administration, and student body resources in this way, significant attitudinal changes in the perception of students with learning disabilities can be generated at the graduate and professional school level.

The reason for so few programs at the highest levels to help students with learning disabilities may be more complex than the existence of prejudicial attitudes of a few educators and administrators. Increased cost factors have to be considered. In addition, an erroneous perception is held by some that students with learning disabilities are receiving preferential treatment. This may lead to jealousy and a morale problem in the student body.

The core mission of educators must be to teach the curriculum to students effectively. For the student with learning disabilities, this means that the diagnosis must be complete, proper methods of instruction and assessment must be emphasized, and the treatment reliable and useful. Our success in this mission will result in securing a more meaningful and successful educational experience for students at the graduate and professional school level. It will also help them develop future learning techniques. We know that the learning disabled, for the most part, have special talents that can be used to achieve success. These talents must be identified and developed.

Something scarcer, finer, and rarer than talent exists. It is the ability to recognize talent. Those involved with the education of the learning disabled have the responsibility of identifying these talents and gently persuading these students to develop their potential strengths further. This is the mission of a post-secondary faculty. It is these untapped strengths and their identification that will enable the learning disabled to realize their goals. Educators must teach! Educators must also realize that the essential objective is to determine what the student knows about the subject. The habit of giving examinations in a prescribed amount of time must be reviewed and in certain instances eliminated. This general type of examination does not accurately measure each student's knowledge. Some students think faster than others, but not necessarily more accurately. Time limited examinations give faster students an edge. An examination that is not time limited would give a more accurate picture of a student's ability. Timed examinations simply reveal how much a student can recite about the subject within a prescribed time.

The strength and heart of any educational institution are its dedicated and talented faculty. Teaching requires special skills. Teaching is communication and part of communication are words. The word is the skin of an idea. The faculty must learn how to communicate ideas to their students with learning disabilities and help these students develop a learning style. It is a simple formula. We teach learning styles, the student practices, practice becomes habit, and habit develops into a skill. This formula rarely fails.

Clearly, students with learning disabilities must be recognized as individuals who have great potential and can add immeasurably to the diversity and overall value of any academic program. We must understand that any accommodation afforded them is not a privilege but a right. We are simply leveling the playing field. It is incumbent upon educators to erase the implication, and resultant injustice, that arises from the notion held by many that a student with a learning disability has limited ability. Ultimately, it is the responsibility of administrators to provide each student with the appropriate support necessary for that student to achieve his potential.

Students with learning disabilities at every academic level can and do learn! They can and do succeed! They can and do become contributing members of their profession and society. The greatest impact of a learning disability program lies, not in any statistic, but in the emotional well being, improved self-esteem, and success of these students. There are moments in our lives when we can make a difference in the lives of others. When this moment arrives we must seize it for it will have a profound effect, not only on those we help, but ultimately on ourselves and society.

Faculty Issues-

A supportive faculty is essential to a successful learning disability program. Frequently, the clinical faculty in a professional school is more supportive than the didactic faculty. There are several reasons for the differing attitudes:

1. Clinical faculties, though they use finite grades, really work under the concept of acceptable or unacceptable performance. However, the didactic faculty

works under finite conditions, where the answer to a multiple-choice type question is exactly two points, or three points. The didactic faculty has retained the outdated nineteenth century, rugged individualism attitude that giving extra time on examinations is an unfair advantage for students with learning disabilities. Two learned research papers have revealed that additional time on an examination gives no unfair advantage to students with learning disabilities but recognizes that there is no essential relationship between speed and knowledge.[1]

    2. Some academic faculty at the graduate and professional school level prefer research or other scholarly endeavor to teaching. However, educators have the moral obligation to teach effectively and supply the information necessary to help make students successful. Clearly, tenure or academic freedom should not be a protective barrier, insulating an uninterested or uncommitted faculty against providing appropriate accommodations for the learning disabled.

    3. Clinical faculties have much greater exposure to the general population through their training and private practices. They are better trained to deal with differences

---

1 "The Validity of the Use of Extended and Un-Timed Testing for Post-Secondary Students with Learning Disabilities" is a doctoral dissertation written in 1993 by Dr. Susan Weaver. The other paper, entitled, "The Effect of Extra Time on Reading Comprehension Scores for University Students With and Without Learning Disabilities" is written by M. Kay Runion.

in people than their academic peers, since they usually develop a better understanding of the general population. Subsequently, they are more attuned to the problems of the learning disabled. Often, the didactic faculty feels that they, "do not know much about learning disabilities and do not care." Not only is this inappropriate attitude, but its practice borders on malfeasance.

Unfortunately, negative perceptions continue to exist among educators and administrators toward the learning disabled. Many still believe that students with learning disabilities are not able to understand and learn at the same capacity as their peers, especially at the graduate and professional school level. Some educators feel that any additional time necessary to teach these students is wasteful. Often I have heard the question asked by faculty, "Who needs them?" The question reflects a prevailing attitude. It is based on faculty misconceptions about learning disabilities. Disregard for students is the first characteristic of incompetence.

One basic problem at the graduate and professional school level is the lack of knowledge and educational training by faculty and administrators in the field of learning disabilities. College is a trust, and the faculty and administrators are trustees. Both the trust and trustees are created for the benefit of the students. Realistically, administrators and faculty should be skilled and competent professionals, knowledgeable about the new teaching strategies and the law supported services applicable to students with learning disabilities. They should be acquainted with the comprehensive methods of assessment, student satisfaction, and other educational outcomes related to the field of learning disabilities. There remains a continuing need for educating faculty and administrators to eliminate the false impression that a student with a learning disability has limited ability. We must change this erroneous belief that the ability to do well on examinations is the sole indicator of a "better" student and that going through the process of taking examinations makes students "better." One central objective of the NYUCD program was preparing the faculty to understand students with learning disabilities and help them learn. The faculty at graduate and professional schools should understand the various ways students learn. The costs of social and personal failure are too great for our society not to use all available knowledge, skill, and resources to press vigorously toward solutions of the problem. Armed with this kind of conceptual knowledge, the faculty would be genuinely empowered. They would understand how each student is progressing and implement the proper support mechanisms.

Graduate and professional faculty have little training in the methodology involved in "educating" students. Typically, they present the student with information and expect the student to process this information, recite it back on examinations, and, hopefully, retain it for future reference. This teaching attitude is archaic! Its time has passed! Those involved in modern education should realize that more is demanded in "educating" students whether or not they are learning disabled. Faculty members at graduate and professional schools must be better equipped "to teach." They need to intervene at the earliest possible moment to avert the chance that students with learning disabilities will fail the curriculum. Research clearly indicates that good teaching can improve student achievement. Educators have the moral obligation to teach and impart the required information to students with learning disabilities. Educators have the additional responsibility to help these students attain their professional goals. Students with learning disabilities have the right to be taught by well-trained faculty who hold high expectations for their students. Experience has shown that as near optimum results can be achieved by students with learning disabilities as by students without learning disabilities with otherwise equivalent capacities. However, in spite of our concerted efforts, not all students succeed. Clearly, some students with learning disabilities will never be "cured" any more than blindness or deafness can be "cured." These students earned the right to be in graduate and professional school and this right is accompanied by the possibility of failure.

Chapter Six

ACCOMMODATIONS _____

Many students with learning disabilities succeeded without taking medical leave and pursuing remediation. For these students, the director discussed the learning disability program at length. The students were advised of the program's advantages and disadvantages. The program offered many support services, namely: receiving special instructions in study strategies, test-taking techniques, methods of self-testing, and appropriate accommodations. The term accommodation generally refers to a change made in testing material or test administration that enables the student to take a test and be assessed with respect to his abilities or skills, rather than his disability. This gave the student with learning disabilities a chance to show his mastery of course material. Accommodations are simply changes in the manner a test is taken, without changing the test content. Other accommodations include such things as increased time to prepare a project; special seating for lectures and examinations; testing in a quiet place; and a reduction in course load.

Graduate and professional schools are required by law to make "reasonable" accommodations for students with learning disabilities and, usually, to assume the costs associated with these accommodations. Accommodations alone will not make these students successful. They are catalysts that help facilitate learning and help the student demonstrate mastery of course content. Accommodations, such as offsite testing or writing a paper instead of taking an examination are often granted in undergraduate college, but are difficult to arrange in graduate and professional school. Accommodations are not designed or intended to lower school standards. The test-giver is not responsible for determining which accommodations are necessary for any particular student. These are determined by the faculty and the student with consideration for each student's learning problem. The most frequently allowed accommodations include:

1. Auxiliary aids such as tape recorders. Although the effectiveness of this accommodation remains open to question, it is one that school administrators readily allow. Tape recorders appear to be effective in helping students with learning disabilities in the lower grades, but they tend to be ineffective support mechanisms in professional schools where information to be mastered is usually presented in daily lectures. There is seldom time to review tapes of lectures after school hours and still prepare for the next day and/or review older material. Additionally, the voice tones and body movements of the lecturer often suggest what is important. This is lost on tape. If the student's academic load can be made lighter by placing him in a five-year program instead of a four-year program, the increased time may make the tape recorder an effective instrument.

2. <u>Textbooks</u> on tape and specialized reading software (computerized readers) are normally allowed when they are available. Not every graduate or professional school provides these accommodations because of the technical expense. Additionally, it is questionable whether sufficient time is available to the student to use these accommodations and whether they would be helpful.

3. <u>Note-takers</u> may be provided by some institutions, although this too is of questionable benefit. It is difficult to learn from another person's notes. The note-taker may use complex, multi-syllabic words which the student with learning disabilities may find difficult to read and remember. Note-takers may use different words for descriptive purposes, thus confusing the student. For example, the note-taker may use the word "arrest" instead of the word "stop," causing the student with learning disabilities to think of the word "arrest" in the legal sense. Additionally, the note-taker may not discriminate what is most important in the lecture.

4. <u>Visual aids</u>, (such as charts and models) which can be very helpful to the student, are not always available. Such aids are expensive, and often irreplaceable. When such aids are available, the chairperson of the department may make an exception and allow the student with a learning problem to use them.

5. Many schools <u>assign lecture seating</u>. Students with learning disabilities should sit close to the lecturer. This position allows for better hearing and the possibility to lip read, a learning strategy many students with auditory

processing problems use. Changing the seating assignment is not an unnecessary burden for the administration.

6.   Students with learning disabilities often need <u>additional time</u> to complete papers and other assignments. Although professors may not always grant it, we advise students to request time extensions. These extensions should always be negotiated in advance by the student and faculty. If possible, a request should be made to the professor for a review of the initial outline and a reading of the first draft for suggestions and comments.

7.   <u>Testing accommodations for students with learning disabilities</u>:

a. <u>Additional time</u> is the most frequently provided accommodation. The time allowed should be at least one-and-one-half times that allowed for non-learning disabled students. Decisions concerning time extensions should be reviewed on a case-by-case basis. Although the concept of unlimited time exists in the law, we have found it often to be detrimental to the student. Being allowed too much time can result in the student changing more right answers than wrong ones.

b. The student should be allowed to take the examination in a <u>quiet room without any distractions</u>. This allows the student to maintain an adequate level of concentration and focus.

c. Some students may need to read aloud to facilitate their comprehension. Others may need a <u>reader</u> to compensate for the student's difficulty in reading the material. The technical vocabulary common in graduate and professional schools require the reader to understand the words and pronounce them correctly. The reader should read throughout with neutral inflection to avoid giving the student any inappropriate signals concerning the importance of the material. The reader must read the material, not interpret it. Readers were used several times in the New York University College of Dentistry with mixed results.

Scribes may be necessary if essay examinations are given or if the student has a reversal problem or becomes confused by the IBM scoring sheet. The scribe's role is to write only what is dictated. Students assisted by a scribe or reader should take the examination in a room separate from other accommodated students to avoid distractions.

d. In certain situations, the time of day and the test schedules can be critical. Some students tire easily because of the energy expended in their daily routine of reading and learning. In these cases, the student should take the examination in the morning. At this time, he has the most energy and he is fully alert. Because of the numerous examinations in professional schools, the student should be accommodated by increasing the time interval between examinations. This will allow the student more time to master the information needed. To accomplish these accommodations, cooperation is necessary from the faculty because it requires constructing more than one examination.

The New York University College of Dentistry program was constantly being fine-tuned. Periodically, the faculty was reminded of their obligations under the law. Sometimes, the faculty was requested to go beyond legal requirements. The concept of "content tutoring" was introduced in a memorandum. (See Appendix B, page 245)

Today, many schools and licensing entities use computer programs for testing. Many of these computers have talking terminals, precluding the need for readers and scribes. However, most of the programs are written so that once a question is answered it cannot be retrieved for review. Chapter Nine will explain the importance of the ability to review questions.

The student was reminded that despite all these efforts success is not guaranteed and he may experience periods of depression upon failing an examination. He may become discouraged with marginal success. The program director reminded the student that success means one step at a time. Success seldom takes place in broad leaps. Success is constantly moving forward; the distance is not critical.

Using time efficiently is a crucial element for success, a basic component for progressing academically: time to read, to learn, to process information and memorize, and additional time to take tests. Learning problems prevent most students from processing all the required information in the allotted time. Therefore, developing compensatory strategies is essential. The implementation of compensatory mechanisms to reduce the time necessary to process and learn information is critical.

Chapter Seven

NOTE-
TAKING

Note-taking is often very difficult for students with learning disabilities. Those with auditory processing problems are particularly affected, but students with visual problems may also be affected. When students with auditory processing problems attend lectures, they frequently improperly process many details presented by the lecturer. Their hearing is fine, but their ability to process sequential language is inefficient, as is their ability to process the beginning or ending sounds of words. For example, they may hear sounds improperly, i.e., "treats" instead of "streets." They may not process plurals and the end syllable of multi-syllabic words. Students with auditory processing problems need additional time to decide which words they want to use. This frustrates their note-taking. Lecturers who speak rapidly, use complex sentences, or speak with an accent present special problems. Students with auditory processing problems have difficulty following a course of conversation with two or more people speaking simultaneously. They may have trouble distinguishing between a concerned and condescending voice. Any interruption while the student is trying to follow the lecture is disconcerting and disruptive. For most students with learning disabilities simply listening to a lecture and trying to select and record the critical points is very demanding . Because these students often use multi-syllabic words incorrectly, their vocabulary tends to be limited. This makes note-taking inefficient because they employ several words where one would suffice.

Students with auditory processing problems may use a number of ways to make note-taking more efficient. Not all of them are practical and some may be inappropriate.

1. *Tape recorders*. The use of tape recorders might be effective in graduate school, but is likely to be a waste of time in professional school where the intense schedule limits time for reviewing tapes. Listening to tapes, students with auditory processing problems would most likely be studying in an area of weakness. Their auditory processing ability is inefficient and unproductive.

2. *Outlines*. When lecture outlines are available, they are usually presented at the beginning of the lecture. This is not very helpful, especially for students with learning disabilities. Professors who provide outlines of future lectures are serving all learners.

3. *Questions*. The student may ask for clarification, repetition, or elaboration of statements made by the lecturer. However, lecturers have a finite amount of material to cover in a prescribed amount of time and such interruptions are disconcerting to the sequence of the material presented. Often they are not tolerated. Asking the lecturer to spell the names of objects during the lecture is also unacceptable. Students, after the lecture, are expected

to research material they do not understand.

4. *Transcripts*. Having a good set of notes is extremely important because the information presented by the lecturer is generally the most important material in the course. Usually, examination questions are based primarily on such information. Since technical books are often outdated the day they are published, current information presented in lectures takes precedence over information found in textbooks.

Lectures and note-taking are usually difficult for students with learning disabilities, but these may be the easiest problems to remedy. Most professional schools have a lecture transcription service that tapes all lectures, transcribes them, and offers them to students for a fee. Occasionally, students run the transcription service themselves to keep costs down. The resulting transcripts are provided to students to help with their note-taking and with understanding the lecture material. Unfortunately, these transcripts are often completed and distributed a few days before and often only hours before the examination. This may accommodate some students, but students with learning disabilities do not do well with last minute studying. Receiving the transcripts a day or so before an exam has limited value for students with learning disabilities.

Inefficient note-taking can be remedied by using transcripts from the previous year and preparing a superior set of notes that will increase learning efficiency.

Information presented by lecturers in professional

schools varies slightly from year to year. In a static science course like Anatomy, variation rarely occurs. Other courses, such as Biochemistry, may vary from year to year, but any new information does not make a significant difference. In a three or five-year period, however, information in this course can vary significantly.

To compensate for note-taking difficulties, students should obtain transcripts from a student who took the course the prior year. In graduate school, there may be several repositories for lecture materials including societies, fraternities, or the library. Since lectures may not be given by the same lecturers each year, the material presented or the emphasis on the material may vary. In professional school, fortunately, course lecturers seldom change from year to year. After acquiring lecture transcripts, students should read them the night before or, at least, several hours before the lecture to get an idea of the material, its organization, and new or unfamiliar technical terms. By reviewing the previous year's transcripts, students can familiarize themselves with new terms before the lecturer uses them; hence, they will be able to concentrate better on the lecture material. In subjects where words are technical and specific to the course, as in science and the professions, previewing words can improve fluency which appears to aid comprehension. Repeated readings of the material are effective in improving reading rate, accuracy, and comprehension. The optimal benefit occurs after three or four readings. Using transcripts in this manner can be very beneficial to students with learning disabilities.

After reading the previous year's transcripts, the student should attend the lecture and concentrate on taking notes, highlighting, especially, any information that did not appear in the prior year's transcripts.

The same day, he should combine the prior year's transcripts and his present notes into one carefully written document. This document should be written legibly, concisely, and in his own words because remembering the words of others is much more difficult than remembering his own. The use of a wordprocessor is very common, but a handwritten document is generally more worthwhile. While the student is rewriting these notes, he is actually studying in a multi-sensory mode, both "reading" the previous material and "writing" the new material. When finished, the student should have an excellent set of notes to be studied for future school examinations and reviewed when taking the licensing examination.

Lectures generally correspond to a chapter in the prescribed course textbook. When melding the transcripts and notes into a final comprehensive study document, the student should also use his textbook. The text book organization can be very useful in constructing an excellent set of notes. This note-taking strategy is extremely useful for all students. For students with learning disabilities, it may mean the difference between success and failure.

Chapter Eight

MYTHS _____

There are several myths concerning students with learning disabilities in graduate and professional schools.

REVERSALS

Many faculty members believe students who reverse numbers and letters are dyslexic and, conversely, that students who do not reverse numbers and letters are not dyslexic. Few students at the graduate or professional school level reverse letters or numbers unless they are under severe time restraints. Since students ascending the academic ladder continuously deal with language and numbers, they develop compensatory mechanisms and strategies that diminish reversals and often cause them to disappear. Put under time restraints, the student with learning disabilities will often revert to reversals, poor spelling, etc. At certain times, even students without learning disabilities will reverse letters and numbers and misspell words. The presence of reversals, by itself, is not an indication of learning disabilities. One of the biggest fears of the faculty at New York University College of Dentistry was that a student with a reversal problem would inadvertently work on the wrong side of the mouth. This happens only when appropriate care is not exercised and can happen to someone without learning disabilities. This problem is overcome by vigilance and, if necessary, by referring to an appropriate marker, such as a watch, always worn on the same arm.

INVISIBLE HANDICAP

The myth of "invisible handicap" derives from the observation by untrained observers that students with learning disabilities appear to perform and act like students without any disabilities. However, the presence of learning disabilities can often be suspected by observing student action and performance: for example, a student who appears intelligent and seems to know the academic material fails examinations despite arduous preparation. The observer's failure to recognize the possibility of a learning disability in such a case reflects poor vision on his part rather than invisibility of the issue. He may deny the existence of the problem and attribute failure to other factors making the handicapping condition 'invisible.'

RETARDATION

This myth suggests that students with learning disabilities are actually retarded. Some believe the label 'learning disability' is employed to gain academic advantages over fellow students. Others consider these students not as retarded or unmotivated but as "educationally" backward and unable to keep pace with their peers. Therefore, they may view graduate or professional school as an unrealistic goal for these students.

VANISHING DISABILITY

This myth proposes that learning disabilities vanish as a student ascends the educational ladder. "How did this student advance so far in academics?" The answer is simple. Students with learning disabilities are unique and resourceful. Many learn to compensate for their problems and work in areas of strength not weakness. These students develop automaticity by repeated exposure to information. Additionally, while ascending the educational strata, students do better because they increasingly work in areas in which they are greatly interested.

COMPENSATION IS A CURE

Another myth declares that "compensated" means cured. As persons with learning disabilities grow to adulthood, there is usually an increase in demand for task accuracy; however, their speed in completing tasks still remains slow. Accuracy alone is an inappropriate measure of disabilities. When placed under time pressure and when the amount of academic material to be learned is extensive, the student with learning disabilities may fail because he does not have sufficient skills, strategies, or compensatory mechanisms to handle information at a higher academic level.

MYTH OF SUCCESS

This myth assumes that all students with learning disabilities can be successful in graduate and professional school with a little help. It further assumes that with this help these students can learn and perform as well as their peers. Another prevailing myth suggests that tutorial assistance alone is sufficient to make these students successful. Such students will still be at a distinct disadvantage without basic skill improvement and accommodations. In graduate and professional schools these students need help to realize their potential.

Learning disabilities persist in a compensated form in adulthood. Frequently retesting a previously diagnosed college student is unnecessary. In fact, the federal courts have held that no need exists to test post-secondary students with learning disabilities more frequently than every five years.

On examinations, dyslexic persons generally rely on context material to understand a question and to choose an appropriate answer, but many educators at graduate and professional schools give students with learning disabilities short answer and multiple-choice type questions. By definition, their context material is minimal. It is obvious if these students are to fulfill their potential, testing accommodations are necessary.

"MILD" LEARNING DISABILITIES

Finally, there is the myth of "mild" learning disabilities. Underlying this myth is the assumption that these students do not need any accommodations. It is the same fallacious reasoning as saying someone is *slightly* pregnant. Consider two people, one 5 feet tall and the other 6 feet tall, each having one leg 4 inches shorter than the other. Both have a disability. Both would be at a disadvantage in a foot race. To know who actually would be at a greater disadvantage is impossible except by some type of physical test, such as a foot race. To give one an accommodation and not the other is inappropriate. A person with a learning disability is entitled to accommodations no matter the severity, especially when no known scientific method of measuring the extent of the disadvantage exists. Even those that appear to have relatively minor disadvantages may still suffer difficulty if their needs are not met. We give glasses to the sight impaired and would not deprive that person of this accommodation during an examination. Why do we deprive the learning disabled of their right to similar accommodations?

PART III

⇒✦⇐

STRATEGIES

Chapter Nine

STUDY
CONCEPTS_____

Few graduate or professional school students have had formal study skills or test-taking courses in high school or college. Students learn these strategies largely through trial and error. Their study requirements may be similar but their study techniques vary. One student might study in the solitude of a quiet room in the dormitory, while another will seek the quiet of a library setting. The requirement is similar, specifically, a quiet atmosphere, but the approach is different. Both students need quiet surroundings, but one also needs to see other individuals in the room in order to feel comfortable. Their learning styles reflect their individual psychological profiles. Many students can develop effective study and test-taking proficiency on their own. Students at graduate and professional schools, especially those with learning disabilities, may find that their prior study and test-taking methods are inadequate to maintain satisfactory grades. Lack of effective learning techniques and test-taking skills is a major cause for poor school performance.

Many excellent texts describing study and test-taking tactics are available. One of the best is by Joan Sedita, formally South Campus Educational Director of The Landmark School, located at Prides Crossing, MA.

These texts are written almost exclusively for students at the secondary and lower school levels. Some texts are directed to post-secondary school students. However, few, if any texts have been written for students at the graduate and professional school level. Study and test-taking strategies are beneficial to all students, both learning disabled and non-learning disabled. The assumption that students without learning disabilities learn these techniques without tutoring is faulty. The study and test-taking methods presented in this text have universal application. Without these approaches, success for students with learning disabilities is problematic.

Study and test-taking strategies are unique to the individual. Some students need constant noise (music), to block out distractions (car horns and/or doors closing). Others require dim light because a bright light is annoying and intrusive on their ability to study. The NYUCD program director advised students to study where they felt comfortable. In the correct location, students will feel relaxed and subsequently be able to concentrate more effectively. Noise is not necessarily a distraction.

Students must be able to master increasingly difficult material. Students, especially those with learning disabilities, who lack sufficient decoding, cognitive and language skills will find such material increasingly difficult to learn. They will probably underachieve academically.

Initially, the program director reviewed the student's study and test-taking methods. When information is learned at an automatic level then the student can rely on remembering it. It is through constant practice and review that automatization occurs. The director made suggestions to enhance the effectiveness of these strategies. Comparing the needs of the student with learning disabilities to those of a baseball player proved to be a model that helped students grasp the need for improved study and test-taking skills. A baseball player might be an excellent hitter in high school where the pitchers are not necessarily very good. Our hypothetical player is strong, game smart, and has a good batting average. Based on his demonstrated ability, he might receive a college baseball scholarship. In college, he remains a respectable hitter but his batting average falters and falls. In college, the pitchers are bigger, stronger, and uniformly better. He has difficulty hitting a curve ball. It becomes more difficult for him to maintain a respectable batting average using only his intelligence and available skills. Based on his overall abilities, our hypothetical baseball player is selected in the professional baseball draft and sent to the minor leagues for seasoning. Here the pitchers are even better, bigger, stronger, and some use the curve ball effectively. He maintains a respectable batting average by hitting fast balls but he still cannot compensate and hit the curve ball. Eventually, he is called up to the major leagues. Here he begins to fail dramatically. At this level, almost every pitcher has a good curve ball. Unfortunately, he has not acquired the skill to hit this type of pitch. If he does not develop a compensating mechanism or affect some change allowing him to hit the curve ball, he will not remain in the major leagues. He will ultimately fail.

The analogy is simple. In graduate or professional school, the massive amount of information to be processed and stored in the brain is comparable to facing the challenge of the curve ball. At the undergraduate level, our student did not encounter in each course such amounts of material to be learned, stored, and retrieved. Perhaps in an occasional undergraduate course, he faced this challenge. He is similar to our baseball player who may have faced an occasional pitcher with a curve ball at college.

ORGANIZATION AND STRUCTURE

Students with learning disabilities are often disorganized and unstructured. This can be fatal in any academic arena especially in graduate and professional school.

Organizational methods

"Straight" and "global" are the two most common methods of organization. "Straight" organization, the most generally employed, uses an alphabetized system in which titles are given to separate and distinct entities and these are filed alphabetically in folders and are placed in a filing receptacle, such as a cabinet. For example, in this system, a file for Anatomy, Biochemistry, Physiology, etc., is instituted. Professionals believe this is the best method of creating structure and organization, especially when numerous papers and distinct entities are involved. This is not necessarily the best for all students. Students with learning disabilities may have difficulty remembering titles given to particular folders and therefore waste a great deal of time trying to retrieve information.

In "global" type organization, papers are assembled in groups based on themes. For those that are adept at "global" organization, articles that need to be read do not necessarily need to be placed in a folder in an alphabetical filing system. If the student has "global" organizational skills, he will know where these articles have been placed, since, placing them in a particular group for him is entirely logical. One group might consist of correspondence awaiting responses or papers that need to be read or reviewed. Another group might consist of documents needing additional information before any response can be made. At times, papers may be placed in the wrong group but misfiling also occurs.

"Straight" organization is probably the best solution to structure and saving time. However, it is often disastrous to try to make every person a "straight" organizational practitioner, especially if he has been a "global" organizer for a protracted period. It is difficult to convince students without organizational skills that keeping their lecture notes sequentially in folders and filed alphabetically would make their studying easier and more efficient. Occasionally, students can be taught to maintain an alphabetized filing system while placing two or three more frequently used folders to the front of the file so that they do not have to go through the entire filing system to retrieve the needed category. This practice might be considered a combination of the "global" and "straight" organizational systems.

For all people, modifying behavior is difficult; for the student with learning disabilities it is often extremely difficult. To be sure that the student understands the necessity of organizational skills, we need to provide constant review. Often, changing behaviors is the most important step toward success for the student with learning disabilities

As the student uses time more efficiently, his productivity increases. He may use a calendar for long and short range planning, for daily activities, for noting test dates and times, for assignment dates, and for other important functions. Using a large calendar gives the viewer a clearer perspective. A compartmentalized attache case or book bag should be used to transport books or papers. Needed material can then be separated and accessed quickly, saving time.

Organizing study time is also important. The student should allocate the same number of hours each day for studying. There is a considerable difference in the work load between undergraduate college and graduate and professional school. Because of the increased volume of material to be learned in graduate and professional school, the student must reevaluate study time requirements. If the student decides that four hours per day is the minimum time necessary to learn at the graduate or professional school level, he should not alter this unit unless he seeks to increase it. Study time always comes before recreational time, but students need some recreational time. We must allow the brain time to process and store information during rest periods. Working slowly and accurately is best. Speed results in inaccuracy and inefficiency. When study time is limited, switching from subject to subject with rest intervals in between is efficient and effective. (See Space Training, page 133). Usually, weekends allow for longer study time; therefore, taking breaks or rest intervals is imperative. In fact, the breaks should involve aerobics, such as playing an active sport (basketball) or brisk walking. Students with learning disabilities usually have no overdrive. They cannot "turn it up a notch" or "cram" for examinations and expect to be efficient. Spare time is spent reviewing course content. Constantly repeating material allows the student to automatize information and be better prepared for examinations

Several students in the NYUCD learning disability program had IQ's below 100. Test results indicated reading at the fourth and fifth grade level. It is virtually impossible for a student with learning disabilities and a true IQ score of 100 or less to be admitted to dental school. We may assume that the low IQ reflects the timed nature of the tests. The reading scores simply mean the student was only able to read at these levels *in a prescribed amount of time*. However, reading test scores at the fourth or fifth grade level do not mean that the student cannot understand the material. If his true IQ is sufficient, he has the inherent ability to understand. He probably must spend more time than his non-learning disabled peers in reading and re-reading. His ability to comprehend may be impaired by difficulties in automatic word recognition. Even mild difficulties detract from the meaning of words and sentences, reduce the speed of reading, and create the need for re-reading the passages. As the student's study efficiency improves, he will find additional time for reading slowly and re-reading assignments.

Finally, the student should determine how and what to study prior to examinations when he will need to add to the time he has allotted for daily study. With the added time, the student can continue the daily study of his other courses while spending more time on the course to be examined. The student cannot afford to stop studying the other courses. To automatize information, constant review of all courses must be maintained. In this fashion, information is constantly being refreshed in memory and will become automatic.

If the student normally studies four hours a night, this should be increased by at least one additional hour or 25 percent of the previous study time. Where the student is studying several courses during each four-hour study session, he would continue to study these other courses, but only for two hours. The remaining three hours should be devoted to studying for the next examination. With this schedule, the student keeps course information fresh in his mind but places emphasis on the material for the next examination.

Stopping all course study and only preparing for the

examination is inefficient. Studying and reviewing information from all courses at each study session helps information become automatized. Continuously studying other material while concentrating on the examination material further contributes to information being automatized.

Time management

The program director at NYUCD reviewed time management with each student. In undergraduate school, most students realized the time allocation needed to process and retrieve information for an examination. However, these time allocations are often inadequate when students face the demands of graduate and professional school. The student, with the program director's assistance, should determine the time needed to study each course properly, for example, more time should be allocated to study for a four-credit course than for a one credit course. Managing and allocating time for each student is predicated on individual study styles and requirements.

After reviewing the recommendations encompassed in the psychoeducational tests, the program director and the student should decide which compensatory mechanisms are likely to be most effective.

Although most students with learning disabilities have difficulty with reading and writing tasks, the degree and scope of their difficulties vary. Deficiencies in underlying processes, whether visual and/or auditory perception, visual motor, sequencing, or integration abilities vary. These deficiencies affect ways of solving problems and completing course work.

If a student is weak in integration and "symbolic mental manipulation" skills, he will have difficulty organizing and holding data in his brain while using that same material to process other information. Visual memory or auditory memory, or both, for rote symbolic information such as labels, diagrams, and vocabulary may be hindered by the disability. Deficiencies in auditory perception may impair the student's ability to absorb lecture information or to take adequate notes. Students with weaknesses in visual-motor skills may require more time when writing, copying, or drawing. Finally, integration deficiencies may make it difficult for students to express, in writing, ideas that he can more readily express verbally. The compensatory mechanisms a student should employ will vary according to his individual strengths and weaknesses.

An effective study plan outlines for the student when to study, how to study, and the time to devote to each course and examination. Without such a plan the student may fail to complete projects and/or he may have insufficient study time for examinations. Although "cramming" is seldom a good way to study for examinations, students without disabilities often succeed with this approach. Because they generally do not process information rapidly, we advised students with learning disabilities not to "cram" for an examination. Those who do so usually find this inefficient. By planning and setting time priorities appropriately, the need to "cram" can be eliminated or, at the least, significantly reduced. "Cramming" is not essential for success. It is simply a tool for those who have not prioritized their time properly. Furthermore, it is inefficient for most students. Proper structure, with appropriate study strategies, can often create additional time to study for examinations properly. The student needs to learn to organize lecture notes and other necessary papers so they can be retrieved in minimal time. If the student has effective organizational skills, we do not want to change or alter these strategies.

For most students, early morning is the optimum time to study and late in the evening the least desirable. Since classes are usually held during the day, studying is normally done in the evening. Metabolism changes and increased fatigue from the day's activities make evening study less efficient. We advised students to create opportunities during the day for study whenever possible.

Students who study after eating a large meal are likely to find that time unproductive. An increased blood flow to the digestive system reduces the blood flow to the brain, which, in turn, decreases the amount of oxygen available to the brain. This may cause overloading to occur more quickly and thus reduce the effectiveness of studying. It is more productive to schedule relaxation time after a large meal.

Another important ingredient for success is adequate sleep. Insufficient sleep causes problems with focus and concentration and lowers the threshold for irritability and frustration. This decreases the student's ability to learn. Additionally, recent research indicates that sleeping brains help to consolidate and improve memory.

Mechanics

Studying in the same place and closely surrounded by the necessary study materials is the ideal situation. The student should face an open space and not a wall. Facing an open space allows for changing eye focus when looking up. When facing a wall, the focal distance will be approximately the same as the working distance. Changing the focus of your eyes helps reduce tension and fatigue. Avoid facing a very bright light because it will be distracting. Lighting should be sufficient to eliminate eye strain when reading. Lights that are too dim cause tiredness.

The study room should not be too warm. This will stimulate sleepiness and reduce studying efficiency. Additionally, the humidity in the room may cause the student some discomfort and affect studying efficiency. Most students work best when the room is cool. Each student must determine the optimum temperature for maximum study productivity. Adequate ventilation is also important. When the air is stale and oxygen depleted, effective studying is diminished.

When studying, students are advised to wear comfortable clothes. If the student sits for long periods, his feet may swell. Tight shoes are distracting so it is preferable not to wear shoes. A properly designed chair makes it easier to maintain good posture and is conducive to effective studying. There should be adequate room for leg movement and for shifting positions easily. The study plan employs several rest intervals.

All clutter should be eliminated, since it is usually distracting and inhibits movement. Only the books and notes actually needed for studying should be at the study site. All other material should be placed on a nearby table within easy reach.

For effective studying, the proper sound level in the room should be determined by the student. Some students need loud noise and others require almost total silence. The use of ear plugs is not recommended, since they may interfere with normal sensations and impede the study process. Ear plugs inhibit the reverbalization that can help reinforce student learning.

Students with learning disabilities come to graduate or professional school with study styles developed earlier. Now they should reevaluate these study styles and alter them to accommodate the increased amount of information to be processed. The primary cause of failure for students with learning disabilities at dental school is their inability or unwillingness to adopt or adapt the suggested study methods to augment their individual learning style.

THE BRAIN

The brain is remarkably plastic. We can learn throughout our lives. Memory is retained in several brain regions from which it can be subsequently retrieved. Memory involves communication among brain cells and is almost synonymous with learning. Both physical and mental exercise is necessary to keep memory sharp. The more the brain is used, the better it functions. Certain types of exercise help the brain to function more effectively. Aerobic exercises, such as walking, appear to benefit the organization and processing of information more than stretching exercises or weight lifting. Why one type of exercise is more beneficial than another is unclear. Physical exercise increases blood flow resulting in increased oxygen levels in the brain. Exercise not only helps create a healthy network of neurons, the working cells of the brain, but reduces stress, which in turn, helps improve memory. Proper diet, especially adequate amounts of carbohydrates that can be converted to glucose, appears to benefit memory. But junk food, loaded with fat, seems to prevent glucose from being used by the brain and therefore interferes with learning and memory. Some fats, such as the n-3 and n-6 fatty acids not found in junk food, appear to be essential for proper brain function. There are large individual variations with respect to nutritional requirements. A well-balanced diet offers the best prospect of providing all the essentials for proper brain function.

The brain, like a muscle, can fatigue. During the

interview, we ask students with learning disabilities if they can do one hundred push-ups and sit-ups. Usually, they respond in the negative. Next, we ask if they could alternately do five push-ups and five sit-ups until one hundred of each is completed. Students are given a preliminary explanation that after prolonged use, muscles become depleted of oxygen and lose their ability to contract. After a rest period, oxygen is restored to the muscles and they can again function properly. If one set of muscles rests while the other set is used this enables the student to do one hundred push-ups and sit-ups. Alternating between push-ups and sit-ups allows the different muscles time to recover from fatigue. The brain works similarly. When a particular part of the brain becomes tired, another part can be employed to continue studying. Students with learning disabilities who understand and accept this concept are most likely to succeed. To avoid the brain tiring, we recommend that students study alternately different subjects or take rest periods during study sessions.

The brain receives information through the five senses. The sense of smell and taste are seldom involved in academic learning. The other three senses, visual, aural (hearing), and kinesthetic (touch) are predominantly used by the brain to process and subsequently store information. Our eyes can distinguish among colors and among sizes of objects. Variations from soft to loud are determined by sound frequencies through our ears. Shapes can be learned from muscles that convey kinesthetic information.

Textures, such as rough or smooth, can be differentiated by the tactile senses. Using the kinesthetic-tactile sense is a critical way for students with learning disabilities to help imprint information in the brain.

Muscles have wonderful memory. Hitting or throwing a baseball or hitting a tennis ball is improved by constant repetition because of muscle memory. Just as our brain can recall the imprint of a face observed through our eyes and the brain can recall a melody heard years ago and long thought forgotten, so too, can our muscles and kinesthetics help imprint memory. Anyone who learned to ride a bike or ice skate as a child and tried again many years later can attest to the influence of kinesthetics on memory.

In courses such as anatomy where names and relationships between body parts must be learned, students with learning disabilities learn best if they can touch rather than merely view the models and specimens. This is a multi-modal method of learning involving more than one sense and is more effective than employing a single mode. Usually, students with learning disabilities learn best and more efficiently from three-dimensional models which can be touched and manipulated to present various views. This cannot be done with drawings which are limited to visual perceptions skills. It is important that information is received by the brain through many paths for that information to become quickly and adeptly automatized. Automatization means learning something so thoroughly that it can be applied consistently with little or no conscious effort. It involves automatic and correct responses to stimuli. Practice is the key to achieving automatization. When something is learned on an automatic level, it can be retrieved from memory and used as a foundation for further learning. Learning to play tennis is a good example. When first learning to play tennis, we have to concentrate and think about every part of the stroke in order to hit the ball properly. However, when the stroke becomes automatic, we no longer have to think about hitting the ball. This allows the brain to think about other factors such as where to hit the ball. For visual courses, such as histology and pathology laboratories, students should repeatedly copy and draw what they see to help remember slides and diagrams. Students should repeatedly write new terms for courses that depend on rote memory.

Deficiencies in visual perception or visual motor skills may make it more difficult for students with learning disabilities to perceive relationships between the parts and the whole in diagrams. Recognizing these relationships may be more difficult if the positions are rotated. Students must develop cognitive approaches for remembering these diagrams. Verbalizing (speaking aloud) a description of the details and their position in relation to the whole is often effective in enhancing memory. Continuous repetition and review of information placed on flash cards is a helpful technique for acquiring and retaining auditory information.

Students should become pro-active in the learning process whether studying alone, in pairs, or in a group. Students with learning disabilities often stay in the background not wanting to make a mistake and fearing to appear stupid. The more students understand, the more confident they become as they devise personal strategies for learning. For example, if they can touch and feel or use models, they will be more confident in the learning process.

Medical and dental schools provide such an opportunity for kinesthetic learning. In anatomy, a cadaver is supplied for a group of students. The task is to dissect the cadaver and learn the position, configuration, and function of the various components of the body. A dissection book supplied to the students dictates the steps to be followed. Usually, the dissecting is divided equally among the students, but the student with learning disabilities will profit by doing more than his normal share of dissecting. Touching and feeling the parts of the cadaver and using the tactile senses is most beneficial to the learning process. Other examples are histology and pathology where the student needs to identify what is observed through a microscope. Tissues on a histology or pathology slide vary in appearance and the ability to identify their characteristics is necessary. One useful learning tactic involves repeatedly drawing the characteristics visible under the microscope. The quality of the drawings is not important. It is the repetition that is helpful to students.

Compensatory techniques vary from student to student and from course to course. Students must use their strengths to develop appropriate compensatory methods.

In review, an effective learning disability program for a graduate or professional school requires:

1. A strong program director/advocate.
2. Screening and identification.
3. Supportive faculty and administration.
4. Support services.

Under support services, an effective program for students with learning disabilities requires:

1. Resources for emotional support.
2. Accommodations, including:
   a. Testing.
   b. Curriculum adjustments.
   c. Tutoring.
   d. Study methods training.
   e. Test-taking training.
   f. Self-testing training.
3. Behavioral modification.
4. Compensatory mechanism development, including:
   a. Verbalization.
   b. Multi-sensory.
   c. Tactile or kinesthetic.

Several sources of academic difficulty for students with learning disabilities have been identified. The factors contributing to these difficulties include: poor time management, inefficient or inadequate study and test-taking techniques, personal problems, poor comprehension, ineffective memory techniques, and lack of motivation.

Creative adjustments in teaching methodology and in the curriculum should be initiated to help ensure student success. These will allow students to learn more effectively and demonstrate, on examinations, their knowledge. If creative adjustments can be devised, the number of these students failing or doing poorly in graduate and professional schools may substantially decrease.

MEMORY

Memory is a term often used synonymously with learning. The components of memory are exposure or encoding, storage, and retrieval of information. Exposure or encoding is the perception and storage is the retention of information in the brain. These follow an information stimulus. Retrieval is the ability to recall or use stored information when needed. It is important to note that encoding and storage occur in various parts of the brain. A stimulus to the brain causes neurons to be activated and to seek out where storage of information has occurred. This may activate recall.

Working memory refers to a system that stores and allows use of stored information. Working memory involves rehearsal or repetition. It can only hold a limited amount of information at any specific period. Because of this factor, forgetting often occurs.

The alternate goal is to place information in *long term memory,* where we store large amounts of information for a long time. Information requires elaborate encoding in order to attain long-term memory status. Although exactly how memory operates remains a mystery, there is growing recognition that exercising both the body and the brain enhances the effectiveness of the neurons essential for memory. Exercising increases the amount of oxygen available to the brain which helps maintain the plasticity of the brain and improves the capability of long term and life-long learning. Memory is a function of the brain that can be developed. As students ascend the educational ladder, they increasingly require rapid recall of stored information.

Students with learning disabilities at the graduate and professional school level generally have good, often superior, cognitive and rational capacities. However, their rote memory and sequencing are frequently poor. With so much information to be processed and stored in memory, the student's goal should be the automatic retrievability of this information. Studying for twelve 20 minute segments with break intervals is more efficient than one 240-minute study session. Constant exposure is essential for information to be stored in long term memory.

RETRIEVAL

Encoding and storage are useless without recall or remembering. Retrieval is the use of stored information; if we cannot recall information, we do not remember it.

In academia, the most important retrieval process is *explicit memory* - the deliberate and conscious recollection of facts. The two basic types of explicit memory are recall and recognition.

Recall involves information retrieval without hints or cues. Essay or fill-in-the-blank responses are examples of recall questions which require the retrieval of information from explicit memory.

Recognition involves the identification of information to which the student has been previously exposed. Multiple-choice and true-false responses are examples of questions requiring recognition.

Frequently, students recognize information presented on examinations that they would not be able to recall. In some cases, possible answers to a question are so close in meaning that they become confusing to the student. In other cases, recall is better than recognition regardless of the type of examination question. The student must learn to use both recall and recognition. Additionally, during an examination the student must learn to recognize clues that will help him to recall or retrieve information. These are known as *retrieval cues*.

MEMORY TECHNIQUES

Repeat, repeat, and repeat should be most students' touchstone for studying at all academic levels. The more frequently the brain receives the same information, the greater the opportunity for the brain to store this material, and eventually to retrieve it. Repeating information aloud helps the student remember, as does writing information on a piece of paper. Whenever the information is written, the student should use his own words. This makes recall easier. However, simple repetition usually does not aid long-term retention. Long-term memory involves not only repetition but thinking about the information and establishing meaningful associations. We are more likely to recall information if we think about the information purposefully. Learning and recall will improve if ideas are grouped into meaningful categories. Memory skills can improve if the action of a muscle can be related meaningfully to a particular sport or other function. For example, the action of the Biceps muscle can be related to doing chin-ups or the Masseter muscle can be related to forceful closure of the mouth during chewing.

While studying, the student should try to pose questions that might be on the examination and then organize responses to these questions. Writing possible questions and reviewing them at the end of the study session may be extremely helpful. Automatizing information can be made easier by relating what is to be remembered with some person or event that occurred in the student's life. This association will not only make learning more effective but will improve recall.

The art of studying is the most important component for student success. The ability to score well on examinations is fundamental to a successful academic career. If information cannot be processed, stored in the brain, and then retrieved expeditiously, it is nearly impossible to do well on examinations.

STUDYING

There are several studying techniques students find useful. One such approach involves studying: 1) alone, 2) with another student (pairs), or 3) in a group setting. Studying all three ways may be beneficial for the student with learning disabilities, depending on the available time. However, only the student can determine which studying tactic will be most effective. When study time is scarce, studying alone may prove to be the most valuable. If the student requires intervals of absolute quiet, the group setting might be problematic and consequently unproductive. Studying in pairs may prove more beneficial for this student, since moments of quiet would be interspersed with moments of conversation with the study partner. When studying alone, the student has complete control of the setting and the environment.

Alone

A student should allocate time to study alone, for this provides the best opportunity to process, absorb, and automatize the greatest amount of information in a given time. When a student is aware of his learning style and why certain methods are beneficial, he will be more likely to apply these techniques when working independently. The student should select a particular area conducive to studying. Additionally, he must allocate sufficient time to learn the required information. To study effectively and efficiently, the required information must be readily available. Valuable study time is lost if the student, while studying, must constantly move around to secure necessary material. Furthermore, a studying pattern is established when studying begins. This pattern is interrupted when the student has to retrieve additional information. Studying alone permits the student with learning disabilities to manage both the time allotted and the potential problem of "overloading" more effectively. (See page 135).

Pairs

After the student has processed, absorbed, and automatized the required information, having one or more study sessions with a partner can be beneficial. While it is not always possible, it is preferable that the student's partner be a more successful student. Studying with such a partner will help to eliminate or reduce any informational errors that the student acquired while studying alone. Furthermore, this studying technique will ascertain whether sufficient material has been covered to be successful on examinations. Studying in pairs also helps reduce stress caused by the inordinate amount of information needed to be learned. The study partner may have the information needed by the student, thus reducing his anxiety and stress. Studying with a partner also helps reduce the stress caused by the adjustment from college to professional school, especially in the freshman year. Together, the partners can support each other while trying to make the necessary adjustments for professional school.

Problems may occur when studying in pairs. Location must be taken into consideration to avoid distractions that may interfere with the learning process. When studying in pairs, students with learning disabilities usually cannot assimilate the information as rapidly as their non-disabled peers. This may cause them to fall behind and negate the potential advantage of this type of study session. On the other hand, non-learning disabled students may become anxious and frustrated because they have to slow down and wait for their disabled peer. Students with learning disabilities seem to learn best when their study sessions are structured, systematic, sequential, and cumulative. This is seldom the case when studying in pairs. Additionally, students with learning disabilities are more successful in controlling the problems of an overload when they study alone.

Studying with a partner should not be undertaken shortly before an examination. To be effective, studying with a partner requires adequate time for the student to absorb and process information not acquired while studying alone. Therefore, several pair sessions are necessary.

In order for the studying strategy to be successful, the study partner should know about the student's learning disability and the student's learning strengths and weaknesses. The partner must be willing to accommodate for the student's learning style if the study sessions are to be meaningful and effective. For instance, if the student has an auditory processing problem, the benefits of studying in pairs will be greatly diminished if most of the study time is spent in discussing the information. In this situation, the study time will be more advantageous if demonstrations, drawings, or written answers are used when responding to questions from a study partner.

Peer- tutors

The learning disability program at NYUCD developed the concept of "peer-tutors," which involved matching an upper class student with learning disabilities with a lower class student having academic difficulties. They were matched so the two students had the same or similar learning problem. Wherever possible, an upperclassman was selected who was proficient in that particular subject. Consequently, the upperclassman understood and appreciated the problem(s) of the study partner. Having already successfully developed compensatory and bypass mechanisms, the upperclassman conveyed these methods and techniques to the student. Peer-tutoring was intended to complement faculty instruction rather than to substitute for it. The lowerclassman had the option of adopting or adapting to those successful learning strategies acquired by the tutor. In this manner, role modeling proved very effective. When we could not match the tutor to the student, we made certain that the tutor was thoroughly informed of the student's studying strengths and weaknesses. This maximized the effectiveness of the tutorial sessions.

The program was very simple, cost free, and did not require elaborate training of the peer-tutors. Such a planned relationship allowed for freedom of expression of the tutored student and helped decrease anxiety by increasing the student's self-esteem. If the peer-tutor and student are matched appropriately, their relationship can help instill confidence in the student with learning disabilities.

Peer-tutors helped students to improve academically and to use time, study techniques, organization of materials, and manual skills more efficiently. Using tutors increased the morale of students providing personalized attention to their needs. These peer-tutors served as an adjunct to the philosophical commitment of the learning disability program to produce successful dental students and competent dental practitioners. Tutoring was always voluntary for both the student and peer-tutor. The success of students was enhanced by cooperative learning.

The use of peer-tutors had an additional benefit. It provided opportunities for the tutor's personal and professional development. In the course of providing reinforcement of learned material and increasing self-esteem for the tutor, it also increased his confidence. Additionally, it gave the tutor increased exposure to the information, thus helping him further automatize the material. This is an extremely helpful review when studying for the licensing examination.

Group setting

Studying in a group setting with students of different academic abilities helps the student with learning disabilities. He can assess the quantity and quality of information that he has already acquired compared to other students. In studying sessions, the student with learning disabilities must be willing to ask members of the group questions about facts and concepts that he does not understand. The group setting is used to determine the extent of the information needed to be learned. After participating in the group setting, the student then returns to studying alone. This time is needed to master information not previously learned. Studies indicate that students who do some studying in small groups do better than students who only study alone.

OVERLOAD AND SPACE TRAINING

Another study skill is recognizing and reacting to the concepts of overload and space training. When studying, students with learning disabilities tend to "overload" quickly. An overload is the difficulty or inability to process information during protracted studying time. It occurs when the brain becomes tired and is unable to accept additional information. The brain needs rest before it can absorb and process any additional information. In a sense, the brain reacts like a muscle when it is worked too hard or too long. It tires. The key to improving a student's long-lasting memory is the use of a learning technique called "space training." Space training involves study sessions that incorporate rest intervals. This strategy produces stronger and longer-lasting retention of information than the same number of study sessions without rest periods. This phenomenon has been known for over a century. It was first described in 1885 by Hermann Ebbinghaus, a German psychologist.

Ebbinghaus discovered that he could memorize more efficiently by spacing out learning lessons with rest intervals in-between, rather than studying the subject repeatedly without a break. The phenomenon of space training has been corroborated by Tim Tully and Jerry Yin working at the Cold Spring Harbor Laboratory on Long Island, in the United States. They demonstrated that fruit flies learned more tasks when given rest intervals as opposed to those not given rest intervals. The key to the discovery is a molecule called CREB. It appears to act as the master memory switch that sets off the synthesis of proteins which supports the growth of new connections between nerve cells.

Students in the program were taught to recognize overload signals. An overload causes studying inefficiency. Students were advised to take a break and stop studying that particular subject when an overload signal occurs. Many students felt insecure concerning the break period while studying, even about taking short breaks. They believed valuable learning time was lost. The approach is simple. Students should nonetheless stop studying that particular subject and study another type of subject. For example, the overloaded student who was studying anatomy (substantially memorization) stops, then studies a course that is not purely memorization, such as bacteriology.

Neurobiologists recognize many kinds of memory within the brain, each using different anatomical pathways. Memory consists of many interacting systems and subsystems that are different. Studying a new course will involve the use of parts of the brain that are not overloaded. This is similar to the concept of alternating push-ups and sit-ups. Short rest intervals should be interspersed in all study sessions to maximize learning. Lengthy study sessions should incorporate non-study time or recreational time in the routine.

The technique of space training is beneficial in graduate and professional school because it improves both study efficiency and the ability of students to learn more in a given unit of time. It appears that short study sessions separated by rest allows time for the memory activator to recover and enables the brain to operate efficiently for another study session. This is why cramming seldom works.

Overload signals

An overload signal may occur before the student is ready to take the rest interval. To be study efficient, the student must be able to recognize these signals. If the signal is not recognized, the brain will still allow the student to continue studying. However, the absorption and processing of information will stop or be substantially reduced. For example, consider a container (the brain) filled with clear water (information already filed and processed in the brain) and a cup filled with blue water (new information). Trying to pour blue water into the full container containing the clear water will cause the blue water to cascade over the sides. Very little, if any, blue water will remain in the container with the clear water. It is already filled. This is what happens when the brain is overloaded and the student continues studying. In this situation, the brain may permit reading, writing, and other study functions to continue but allows little, if any, of this additional information to be processed for storage in memory.

Overload signals vary from student to student, from time to time, and from subject to subject. One student may become overloaded in a half hour while another in fifteen minutes. The material being studied may affect the time it takes to reach overload. If the student enjoys the course, an overload may not occur as quickly because his interest causes an improvement in focus and concentration and seems to delay an overload. The opposite is true if the student dislikes the course or the information is boring. Each student should make a concerted effort to recognize his overload signals.

Common signals of an overload include:

1. After eating a light meal which satisfies hunger, the student begins to study. After studying for a short time, the student feels famished. This is an overload signal. The remedy is to take a break or rest interval. If the student is very anxious or time is pressing, he should study another subject. For example, if studying Anatomy (a memory course), he should stop and begin studying another course involving conceptualization which employs another part of the brain. An alternate strategy is to eat an apple or other food. This affords the student a rest interval and also satisfies the immediate desire to eat.

2. Following a satisfying nap, the student begins to study. A short time later, he constantly yawns: an overload signal. It is time to begin studying another course or preferably take a rest interval.

3. After studying for a specified time, the student begins to read the same sentences repeatedly: an overload signal.

4. While studying, the student begins having trouble understanding the material. The paragraph is not difficult but the student's ability to understand is compromised: an overload signal. Do not confuse this signal with actually being tired. Even if the student is tired, he should be able to understand and process simple information.

5. The student initiates studying in a quiet place, (at a library or at home), and feels that studying is progressing satisfactorily. Suddenly, the student is distracted by nearly

every sound including the rustling of paper in the library or household noises. This is an overload signal.

6. While studying, the student discovers an inability to remember information recently studied. The student should not become frustrated. The previous information was probably processed by the brain. This overload signal may suggest that a long break is needed.

The overload signal is unique to each individual. It should not be ignored. The student must recognize any variation of the previously mentioned signals. When studying different courses in a particular study session, changing from course to course is an efficient method to learn. Whenever overloaded, the student should place a book mark where he stopped and proceed to another course. If a signal occurs while studying the second course, the student should take a rest interval or return to the previous course. The student can continue studying without loss of information. A rest interval after an overload signal is preferable to switching to study another course. Available time is the criterion.

When preparing for exams, most students feel more comfortable studying several days before the examination and continuing without interruption until the exam. This is understandable but an erroneous strategy. Efficiency and effectiveness occur when the student takes rest intervals or switches to another course when overloaded. The most successful students with learning disabilities in dental school practice the techniques of overload and space training.

Chapter Ten

TEST-TAKING TECHNIQUES

Success in most academic programs is dependent on a student's ability to answer questions accurately on examinations. Examinations may be oral, written, or a practical. As faculty members work with students with learning disabilities, they should share a common goal: to assess what the student knows about the course. It is important for the faculty to have a basic understanding of learning disabilities and the adaptations necessary to accommodate these students. The form of examination used to ascertain the student's knowledge should, in fact, do so. Students with learning disabilities may have difficulty demonstrating their knowledge through traditional means of assessment. In the health professions, and to some extent in other professions, the predominant method of testing is the multiple-choice type question.

There are several logical reasons employed to validate the use of multiple-choice type questions on examinations: (1) it is considerably less subjective than essay and oral examinations; (2) grading is easier, since it is usually machine-scored; (3) the time needed to grade the exam is reduced; (4) it is easier to avoid difficult or poorly constructed questions; (5) it is easier to read, since the student is not writing long answers. The answer is simply reduced to filling in a blank or selecting a presented answer; (6) usually, support staff can grade the exam; and (7) many test constructors believe that this format best trains students to deal rapidly and simultaneously with many different details, for example, dealing with the many factors that may occur rapidly during an emergency. However, empirical evidence does not support the theory that the ability to do well on multiple-choice type questions results in a more knowledgeable or effective professional.

When taking this type of examination, students with learning disabilities report feelings of anxiety, apprehension, confusion, frustration, and a lack of confidence. They complain of being easily distracted, losing concentration, and difficulty in focusing on small details for long periods. Words such as "but" and "or" often go unnoticed changing the meaning of the question for these students. This problem results from the enormous psychological energy expended by students with learning disabilities in continuously decoding the question. This subsequently interferes with their comprehension. Fatigue becomes a major contributing factor in their inability to do well on examinations. Only motivation and a strong desire to succeed can overcome this fatigue.

The difficulty in attention, perception, comprehension, memory, and the process of selecting the most appropriate response continues to make the multiple-choice type question one of the more difficult assessment examinations for students with learning disabilities. Additionally, multiple-choice type questions are frequently framed so that some answers are very close to the correct one. They are referred to as "distractors." This closeness adds to the student's difficulty and confusion.

The following test-taking strategies are helpful to all students but especially to students with learning disabilities:

1. *Relaxation* - An anxious student taking an examination is unlikely to do well. Some anxiety is productive, since it provides a stimulus with the release of adrenalin for the student. However, heightened anxiety often interferes with the retrieval of information because it may cause blocked or compulsive behavior. Anxiety and apprehension are often compounding factors that interfere with the ability of students with learning disabilities to focus attention on small details for long periods.

A student should relax before and during examinations. This may be difficult to achieve, especially if the student is doing poorly or failing the course. A confident student who studied appropriately should not be overly anxious unless this is a facet of his personality. Before the examination begins, the student should focus on something relaxing. He should consciously take deep breaths from time to time and think about relaxing his back, neck, and shoulder muscles. This may help increase confidence and dispel some anxiety.

Except for an essay examination, the student should not glance through the test booklet before or during the examination because he may notice only difficult questions, thus increasing his anxiety level. When taking an essay examination, the student should quickly look over all the questions. This allows him to determine the number of questions that must be answered, the point value of each question, and the amount of time necessary to answer each question.

Other than essay type examinations, the student should start with the first question and continue sequentially. Sometimes the beginning questions are the most difficult. Examinations usually do not contain only hard questions. If all the questions are difficult, they are difficult for the majority of the students. If the first few questions are very difficult, the following questions may be easier. Knowing the course content and following the prescribed test-taking techniques will give the student the basic process for success.

Some students may be unable to control the level of anxiety so that it interferes with their ability to take the examination. Such students should be referred to the appropriate professionals for instruction in relaxation techniques. If anxiety is a major factor, then relaxation is an important step in helping to resolve or minimize the problem.

2. *Quiet place* - students with learning disabilities have difficulty focusing and concentrating on information retrieval; therefore, they should always take examinations in a quiet place. Noise or disturbances cause these students to lose their train of thought and interferes with the retrieval process. A faculty room with persistent traffic where the faculty take their breaks is a very poor

examination site. The room selected should be devoted exclusively to examinations. Furthermore, proctors should not read newspapers or make any disturbing noises since this can be disconcerting and disturbing to students taking an examination.

3. *Adequate pencils, marking pens, and erasers* - Sufficient sharpened pencils with good erasers should be brought to the examination room to avoid loss of time due to broken pencil points. A protracted waiting time for a replacement pencil can further heighten existing anxiety. Anything that can reduce stress and anxiety may help test performance.

4. *Three-by-five filing cards* - Students should bring several three-by-five filing cards to written examinations on which they can record thoughts concerning the examination questions. Often, when reading questions, possible answers occur immediately. These should be noted on the filing cards. The immediate responses should be given strong consideration when answering the questions since they are usually correct. Before the examination begins, the proctor's permission should be obtained to use the cards, so that their use will not be considered suspicious.

5. *Appropriate seating* - The student should sit in the middle of the front row if taking the examination in a room with a group. If examination seats are assigned, the student should petition the administration for a change in the seating assignment. Students who complete the examination early may cause a disturbance when leaving

the room. This can be very disruptive and result in a loss of concentration for the student with learning disabilities. Appropriate seating will minimize the effect of these disturbances on the student.

If the relevant information has not been stored in the brain for quick retrieval, success on examinations will be problematic. Mastery of test content is the best predictor of test success. Once the information is stored in the brain and the student is ready for the examination, many methods can be employed to maximize results. For students with learning disabilities, test-taking techniques will often make the difference between passing and failing.

EXAMINATION TYPES

Practical examinations - Practical examinations, frequently given in graduate and professional schools, especially in science courses, are designed to measure the student's ability to recognize or identify specific parts of animal specimens or cadavers. Other practical examinations are given to measure the student's ability to perform tasks. For example, practical examinations in dental school are used to determine if students can properly prepare teeth to receive fillings or to ascertain if a particular type of impression of the mouth can be made correctly. The accommodation of additional time to take a practical examination can easily be given to students with learning disabilities. Unfortunately, the professional school faculty often opposes the concept of additional time for practical examinations. They fear it could have a detrimental impact on the student's future success in private practice and create an economic hardship for the practitioner. Following the strained logic of this argument, some instructors believe that the inability to pass the practical examination in the prescribed time will cause financial failure in private practice.

However, if students cannot pass practical examinations, they cannot graduate from professional school. Therefore, the opportunity to practice their chosen profession would be lost. Also, using additional time in private practice to accomplish a task may reduce income, but does not necessarily cause financial failure. Deadlines do not exist during surgery. Such a concept is repugnant for those providing health care. There is no requirement that a surgeon do a particular operation within a certain amount of time because it may otherwise reduce his income. Furthermore, the professions are predicated on giving patients the best results, not on making more money. The student with learning disabilities may be excellent in doing practical work; it may simply take him a little longer. Should the student be penalized especially since he can do the work as well as or better than his peers? The ability to produce qualified professional work is always the prime consideration. Time is not an initial qualifying factor in a professional career. Increased speed often comes with time and practice. To punish the student with learning disabilities by not providing extra examination time is inappropriate and, in certain instances, may be a violation of law. Offering additional time to students to complete practical examinations presents no particular problem for the faculty.

However, there are exceptions to giving students with learning disabilities extra time on certain practical examinations. A practical examination in Anatomy is different and presents problems for the faculty. In Anatomy, students need to identify structures on a cadaver. In an Anatomy practical examination, tags are placed on different cadaver parts. The student is required to identify these structures. Students move from body to body in a prescribed time, identifying each tagged structure. Allowing students with learning disabilities additional time during this type of practical examination would be extremely disruptive to other students. Students would have to stop and wait while students with learning disabilities used their time extension.

At New York University College of Dentistry, a system was devised that allowed students with learning disabilities to receive time extensions on practical examinations in Anatomy. This system was also instituted in other courses. Additional time was allocated in the following manner. All the students took the practical examination in the prescribed time. If a student with learning disabilities could not identify a structure or was uncertain, he marked the answer sheet with a question mark. After all the students completed the practical examination, students with learning disabilities were allowed to return to those structures identified with a question mark and use their extra time. Additionally, they were allowed to touch and feel the structures to be identified. The use of the tactile sense to identify structures was of significant assistance. It helped the students with learning disabilities to be competitive with their non-learning disabled peers. During the regular time of the examination touching was not permitted, since constant handling could separate the identification tags from the structures.

There were certain restrictions imposed on the manner the extra time could be used. In some instances, we believed that students would be better served if they were given extra time to return to a specific number of structures needing identification. For example, a student could reexamine five questions. He was given five minutes for each tagged item, totaling twenty-five minutes of additional time. In other instances, the twenty-five minutes additional time could be used for any number of questions. Prior to the examination, the method of allocating additional time was optional and negotiated among the student, the program director, and the departmental chairperson.

Oral examinations - Oral examinations are infrequently permitted in graduate and professional schools but always are included as part of the requirements for the Ph.D. This type of examination is extremely difficult for both faculty and student, especially students with learning disabilities. When they are given, a panel, consisting of three faculty members examines each student. Three faculty members are employed to discourage students from claiming prejudice and to help thwart discord among the examiners when grading students. Objectivity is the prime goal of the examiners. However, on the subconscious level, examiners may be influenced by extraneous factors. A student's appearance and mannerisms may be reflected in the final grade. Additionally, one or more of the examiners may have an accent which could further interfere with the student's ability to understand questions and respond appropriately.

Facing three examiners simultaneously can be very intimidating and may cause the student with learning disabilities to stammer or hesitate when responding to questions. This could give the examiners the false impression that the student is unprepared. Anxious students, whether learning disabled or not, should try to avoid oral tests by presenting appropriate arguments to the examiners prior to the examination.

Oral examinations are especially difficult for students with auditory processing problems. These students may not process the question appropriately, and thus give an incorrect response. Oral examinations are extremely difficult for students whose recall ability is poor. Telling the examiners that the answer is on the "tip-of-the-tongue" is not helpful. In a written examination, a fact on the "tip-of-the-tongue" might be recalled at a later moment in the examination.

Specific advice for taking oral examinations

During an oral examination, reply slowly since you need time to process the question and supply the answer. Prior to answering, repeat the question aloud. This will give you additional time to arrive at the appropriate response. If the repeated question is not the question asked, it will alert the examiners who will restate the question in a manner that you can understand.

Before responding to a question, reframe the question in your mind. Using your own words will help you present a better answer. When you respond, the beginning of the response should always employ the exact words used in the question. For example, if the question is, "What is the function of the Trapezius muscle?" the response should start, "The function of the Trapezius muscle is . . . " This technique will help organize the answer. Responses should be short. The examiners will probably sense if you know the answer. If you cannot answer the question say 'pass' and go on to the next question. Ask to return to a passed question if the answer becomes available. Do not feel intimidated if you cannot answer all the questions. The oral examination is similar to a written examination. The format is different and knowing all the answers is desirable but seldom possible.

Written examinations - There are several types of written examinations. These include true-false, fill-in, essay, multiple-choice, comparison, and case-based type questions or any combination of these types. When taking a written examination, read each question completely. Do not make assumptions about what a question will ask. Once a question has been completed, concentrate on the next question. Do not waste mental energy by reevaluating the answer given on the previous question. Be careful with the answer sheet and avoid making clerical-type mistakes.

QUESTION TYPES

True-false questions - (figure 1) True-false questions offer a minimal amount of context and hence are difficult to understand. However, these questions are arguably the easiest type to arrive at a correct response. Guessing, when unsure of the correct answer, will provide a 50-50 chance of being correct. For this reason, true-false questions are used infrequently. Recall plays the primary role in answering these questions. When you do not understand

Figure 1. An antibiotic, appropriately matched to a specific infectious disease and used to combat this infection, cannot cause an iatrogenic reaction.
                    True _____   False _____

Note: In the question, the word <u>cannot</u> must be <u>circled</u> or <u>underlined</u> **boldly** to indicate the response is in the negative. The correct answer would be False. If you are not positive about the correct answer, place a question mark next to the question and continue with the examination.

the question or are unable to answer it, place a question mark adjacent to the question. During the examination, some factor may trigger an answer to the question. If you do not recall an answer by the end of the examination, then guess.

Fill-in questions - (figure 2) Fill-in questions are difficult because they contain a minimal amount of context material. This makes them troublesome to understand and they require recall and word retrieval. Read the question at least three times to ensure that you understand it. When you do not understand the question or are unable to answer it, place a question mark next to the question and follow the instructions presented at the end of the true-false questions section.

> Figure 2. An untoward reaction caused by medical treatment would be considered _____.
> **Note:** The answer is <u>iatrogenic</u>. This type of question is very difficult because the student must know and recall the answer expediently. If you are not positive about the answer, continue with the examination. You can always guess before the end of the examination.

Essay questions - (figure 3) Essay questions are difficult for students with learning disabilities because they involve recall. The student's reading difficulties are exacerbated by minimal informational context in the essay question. To surmount these problems, read each question at least three times for meaning. Read slowly and underline key words. Circling words, like "never," "not," "always," "maybe," etc. with a red pencil focuses attention on the negative or positive structure of the question.

With each reading of the question, make notes on three-by-five filing cards. By the third reading you should understand the question. If there are any special directions pertaining to the manner of answering the question, you need to understand them. If you understand the question after the second reading, read the question a third time to be certain.

At this point, you should understand the question and have made several notations on the filing card. Often, essay examination questions have several "parts" and each part needs to be answered. Note the number of "parts" of the question on the filing card. Try to put the notations in sequence. Then create an outline for the proposed answer.

Figure 3. A patient arrives at the hospital with a severe infection. A blood sample is taken to test for the most appropriate antibiotic. The selected antibiotic is administered to the patient. How might this antibiotic have been produced or synthesized? How might this antibiotic work? Even though this appears to be the most appropriate antibiotic for this infection, could the antibiotic be harmful?

Note: Following the outlined strategies will allow you to provide the best possible answer.

The outline includes an introduction, a body, and a conclusion. The initial time should be used to make the outline concise. Remember, additional time is available.

After completing the outline, use paragraphs to answer the question. Leave out information that is irrelevant. Try to make the paragraphs conform to the outline previously constructed. Restate the question in the introductory sentence of your answer. Start each paragraph with a topic sentence which introduces the topic of that paragraph. Restate the main idea in the concluding sentence(s) and try to tie everything together. Write neatly so the material is readable. If you cannot write neatly then print. When the question is completed, go on to the next question.

If you do not understand the question or directions, proceed to the next question. Do not waste time trying to understand the meaning of the question. This examination strategy is called 'pass.' It allows you to answer those questions you actually know, rather than wasting time on questions you do not understand or cannot answer. Mark those unanswered questions with a question mark. After you answer the questions, return to those with a question mark and try to answer them.

Save some time for proofreading; this will vary with each student. If you have left a question unanswered, take a calculated guess. Points are not subtracted for wrong answers. When proofreading, do not change answers unless you are absolute certain that the new answer is correct. Usually, the first answer is correct.

Multiple-choice type questions - (figure 4,5) Multiple-choice type questions are those most frequently given and they involve reading short sentences, which provides little context for understanding the question. If you have decoding problems they will interfere with your comprehension. Often, you will need several readings to comprehend fully the questions and responses required. You may find it hard to keep the question or a thought in mind (symbolic mental manipulation) while responding.

Answering multiple-choice type questions depends mainly on recognition. The answer to the question is presented with other choices. Because the potential answers are frequently very close in relevance, you may be further confused. However, following the suggestions below may often increase your grade by ten points or more.

1. Use extended time properly when answering multiple-choice type questions. **ADDITIONAL TIME IS NOT INTENDED TO BE USED TO REVIEW ALL THE QUESTIONS AT THE END OF THE EXAMINATION**. The first answer you choose is usually correct. If you review all questions, you may change more correct answers than incorrect ones. Use extra time to read questions more than once. If you do not understand a question, use time left at the end of the examination to make the best guess you can. This strategy will be discussed later in this chapter.

2. Begin the examination when the command is given and turn to the first question. Before looking at the

question, **cover the possible answers** with a three-by-five filing card. This is extremely important. While reading a question, the eyes frequently drift to the possible answers. Seeing these answers may cause you to misinterpret the question and select a wrong answer. **Read each question at least three times**. If you are sure of the answer after the first reading, read the question again. The second reading will ensure that you understood the question thoroughly. Note possible answers on the filing card. After you have **read and understand** the question, uncover the potential answers. Selecting an answer should be made on the basis of positive, almost positive, maybe, not sure, or do not know. **At this point, select an answer only if you are positive**. Otherwise, you should put a question mark next to the question and revisit it before the examination ends.

Examine each potential answer. While proceeding, **eliminate all obviously wrong answers** with a bold, black line so they can no longer interfere with your concentration. If you select an answer that you are certain is correct, note it. Next, check the answer on the file card. Are they the same? If the answers are the same, then this choice has the greatest possibility of being correct - mark it.

If, while reading the answer choices you are not absolutely certain but almost positive, make a check mark next to this possible answer. After looking at all the possible answers, you will have either picked one answer (a positive choice) or picked more than one possible answer. However, all obviously wrong answers will have been eliminated. This strategy is termed 'POE' - process of elimination.

After three readings, if you still do not understood a question do not examine the answer choices, for doing so may further confuse you. **If you do not understood a question, you cannot answer it properly, except by guessing.** At this point, place a **question mark** next to this question.

Sometimes you may understand a question but be **unable to retrieve the answer** immediately. Place a **question mark** next to this question. A word or sentence from a subsequent question may trigger a response. When you leave a question unanswered, the brain subconsciously often continues to search for an answer, an action similar to the "tip-of-the-tongue" phenomenon. When you guess, the brain assumes the question is completed and no longer searches for an answer. At this point, do not choose an answer by guessing. **Guessing should be done at the end of the examination**. We will discuss unanswered questions later.

3. **Circle signal words** in the question such as "not," "never," "but," "may," "always," "sometimes," "exception," "except," etc. **with a red pencil**. Note words that indicate the question is negative, almost impossible in occurrence, or are very permissive. Such words signal the need to examine the question very carefully for subtle meaning.

4. If you had problems with **reversals** in the past, they are less likely to occur as you ascend the academic ladder. Years of academics have provided you with the opportunity to automatize the sequence and configuration of letters and numbers. However, even with time extensions on examinations, reversals may occur when you are under pressure. On multiple-choice type questions, answers are often noted by the letters a, b, c, d, e, and f. Inadvertent reversals may occur when transcribing answers to the IBM score card. The "b" may become a "d" or vice versa. Sometimes the "c" and "e" are confused. Be especially careful when copying the letter answers to the IBM card. This will help preclude any mistakes made during transposition. Always put the selected letter answer next to the question in the examination booklet. If reversals still occur, arrange for the chairperson or his representative to review your examination booklet and accept these answers instead of those placed on the IBM card.

Mistakes occur less frequently if the letters representing each response are uppercase or if numbers are employed. An appeal will occasionally convince the faculty to use only uppercase letters or numbers to represent responses on examinations. If this arrangement cannot be made, convert the letters to numbers during the examination. In this process, a=1, b=2, c=3 and so on. This is easy to do and should help eliminate problems caused by letter reversals.

5. Allocate time before the end of the examination to re-read and to attempt to answer the unanswered questions

Figure 4. The temporalis muscle inserts into the
    A. coronoid process.
    B. condylar process.
    C. fovea of the mandible.
    D. lateral aspect of the mandibular angle.
    E. articular disc of the temporomandibular joint.

Note: The answer is "A." If you are not positive about the correct answer, look for wrong answers and follow the strategies outlined above, especially POE. Return to the question at the end of the examination and guess, if necessary.

easily identified by the question mark. **Do not review completed questions**. Since you have read the question previously three times, this review should not take long. Furthermore, you have **boldly eliminated** wrong choice answers. Having fewer potential responses to review takes less time. Often, a question you did not initially understand becomes clear in the review. In these cases, select the correct answer. Other questions may not trigger any clue to the answer. In these instances, make a **calculated guess**. Instinct may stimulate a particular answer. Mark it. At this point, nothing is lost by guessing. When all obvious wrong answers are eliminated and only two responses remain, there is a fifty-fifty chance of being correct. If three possible responses remain, selecting the correct answer by chance is considerably reduced. We will review the mathematics of guessing at the end of the chapter.

Figure 5. Opiates are CONTRAINDICATED for patients who have which of the following?
    A. Severe head injury.
    B. Bronchial asthma.
    C. Renal dysfunction.
    D. acute myocardial infarction.
Note: Though the word "CONTRAINDICATION" is capitalized, it should still be circled to provide a continued reminder that the question is negative. Follow the suggested strategies to arrive at the correct answer.

Multiple-multiple-choice type questions - (figure 6) These are questions that consist of the question, a list comprising several factors, and an additional list consisting of several possible answers. The final answer consists of one or more choices from the list of factors. It is possible that no combination of factors is correct; this questions would be answered, "None of the above." This type of question is used often in professional schools but infrequently on licensing examinations. It has the same areas of difficulty as multiple-choice type questions and you should approach such questions in the same manner. **Cover the list of factors and possible final answers** and read the question at least three times. If you do not understand it, signal it with a question mark. Proceed to the next question. If you apply the suggestions above, you may find these types of questions easier to answer than regular multiple-choice type questions. By **eliminating wrong answers**, the correct answer often stands out. Eliminating wrong answers usually narrows the choices down to two possible answers. Sometimes, the elimination of all wrong answers leaves only the correct answer. Consequently, you need not have initially known the correct answer.

> Figure 6. Which of the following statements concerning antibiotics are correct?
> 1. acts as a bactericidal agent.
> 2. acts as a bacteriostatic agent.
> 3. can cause an iatrogenic reaction.
> 4. Reacts with the lining of the esophagus when swallowed.
> 5. Can cause anaphylactic shock even if matched with the patients blood sample.
>> A. 1,2,3
>> B. 3,4
>> C. 1,2,3,5
>> D. 1,2,4,5
>> E. all of the above

Note: In this question, answer number 4 is an obviously wrong answer. This will immediately render answers "B," "D," and "E" incorrect. Eliminate them. Looking vertically, note that numbers 1, 2 and 3 are common to the remaining answers. Therefore, you only have to determine whether choice number 5 is correct or incorrect. If you do not know, you can guess before the end of the examination.

Comparison-type questions - (figure 7) This type of question is used frequently in professional schools and on licensing examinations. Each question consists of a statement and a reason. For example, "It can rain on humid days <u>because</u> the sky is gray." The word "**because**" is the separator between the statement and the reason. Such questions can also be written as two sentences. "It can rain on humid days. Whenever it rains, the sky is gray." Students must realize the complex nature of the question and decide the following: whether the statement is true and the reason is true; whether the statement is true and the reason is false; whether the statement is false but the reason is true or both the statement and reason are false. In this example, the statement would be true but the reason false. The sky is not gray during a sun shower.

Often, attached to the end of each statement will be an additional comment asking whether the statement and reason are related or unrelated. Students with poor symbolic mental manipulation have a great deal of difficulty with this type of question. The ability to hold one piece of information in memory while dealing with another piece of information is essential in selecting the correct answer. The lack of this ability makes the question even more difficult.

When choosing an answer for a comparison-type question, you need to deal with the parts of the question individually. First, **determine whether the statement is true or false**. Mark this on a file card. Second, **determine whether the reason is true or false**. Mark this. Finally, **determine whether the statement and reason are related**

or unrelated. Mark this. What is noted on the file card represents the correct answer. Return to the possible answers and **cross out all wrong answers**. Now match the three answers on the file card to the remaining answers to the question. **What is left is the correct answer**.

Figure 7: In treatment planning, health professionals should consider a patient's ethnic identity and heritage **BECAUSE** the patient's cultural background influences the formation of his health-related beliefs and attitudes.

    A. Both the statement and the reason are correct and related.

    B. Both the statement and the reason are correct but **NOT** related.

    C. The statement is correct, but the reason is **NOT.**

    D. The statement is **NOT** correct, but the reason is accurate.

    E. **Neither** the statement **NOR** the reason is correct.

Note: The correct answer is "A." Following the indicated strategies will help you arrive at the appropriate answer.

Case- based questions - This type of examination question is being used more frequently in the health professions. Case-based questions contain the pertinent medical, dental and social history and chief complaint(s) of an actual patient. Appropriate pictures and x-rays are included. The examination consists of any previously discussed question types, e.g., true-false, multiple-choice, etc. Questions are related to the case presented and can be general or specific. Answer these questions by using the techniques previously presented. You may have to review the case presentation repeatedly for pertinent information. Oftentimes, the answer requires only general information. For example, the case presentation may indicate that the patient is allergic to penicillin. This fact may be restated in a question asking about the advisability of giving penicillin to this patient. In this instance, you need not review the case presentation to answer the question. The ability to recognize these general questions will save time for other parts of the examination.

THE MATHEMATICS OF TEST TAKING

In NYUCD, the passing grade for examinations is seventy. To allay student fears, we demonstrated how passing grades on examinations can be achieved mathematically.

We showed each student that knowing only 50 percent of the answers to questions on an examination is sufficient to graduate from dental school, if appropriate test-taking methods are used. All students agreed that knowing only 50 percent of required information was unacceptable, but they were encouraged by knowing they could achieved a passing grade mathematically. This was based on three assumptions.

The <u>first assumption</u>: the student could respond correctly to 50 percent of a one hundred question examination: 50 points.

The <u>second assumption</u>: all obviously wrong answers from each unanswered question could be identified and eliminated leaving only two possible answers.

The <u>third assumption</u>: for the remaining unanswered questions that have been narrowed to two choices, you could flip a coin in the air. There is a mathematical probability of a fifty-fifty chance of being correct. However, this assumption is slightly flawed. In any sequence of tosses, the final tally may not be fifty-fifty, since the theory of outcomes is based on an infinite number of tosses. During the examination, do not flip a coin for the answer but make an educated guess. The guess has a greater probability of being correct if you have some information about the question. Now, if the initial assumptions are correct and you guess correctly 50 percent of the time you will accumulate another twenty-five points (50% of 50 unanswered questions = 25). Of course, this is based on the underlying assumption that you can narrow the answer choices to two. This would give you a grand total of seventy-five points, a passing grade.

Clearly, you should know sufficient material to achieve a passing grade without guessing. Based on our assumptions, your passing grades improve with a greater knowledge of the material. If you know 60 percent of the information, your final grade would be eighty. If you know 70 percent of the information, the final grade would be eighty-five. Passing examinations is enhanced if test-taking techniques are strictly followed.

After completion, you should not dwell upon an examination. No useful purpose is served reflecting on the results. The only exception is reviewing wrong answers. Do not borrow trouble from yesterday. If you failed, nothing can be done about the result. Move on. Concentrate on the task ahead. Putting it all together for the next examination will be frustrating if you constantly think about the prior examination. Effective concentration contributes to success and lack of concentration results in failure.

Chapter Eleven

SELF-
TESTING _____

Self-testing is designed to save time and increase efficiency. It is an effective way to maximize learning, especially rote learning. Self-testing allows you to review information you have already learned while studying new material.

Increased opportunity for student success is predicated on the ability to automatize information for retrieval and to maximize learning by increasing study time efficiency. Most students cannot measure their knowledge about a particular subject. Therefore, they repeatedly study the entire subject matter. Obviously, students waste time studying material they already know. Determining what they actually know about the subject allows students to discriminate and to concentrate on what they do not know. This creates additional time to learn the needed material and to review the material repeatedly; this in turn facilitates automatization.

Students use a variety of methods during study sessions to increase their retention of information in order to pass examinations. While studying, some students write down questions. At the end of the study period, they try to answer the questions to test their retention of the information. Occasionally, these students save the questions for another study period for self-testing. Though this has some merit, it is inefficient. If you cannot answer the question, or recall only part of the answer, then you have to spend valuable time searching for the needed information.

Another ineffective approach is trying to automatize details by constantly thinking and pondering over this information. Because you only review material you already know, this is an inefficient use of your time. Some students constantly write down information, an effective way to achieve automatization of known information. However, you cannot write down information that you do not know. The most important question you can ask is, "What do I know about the subject?" When you determine what you know about a subject and study only what you do not know, you will become more efficient.

There are two effective ways to determine what you know and what you do not know about a particular subject. One involves the use of old examinations and the other involves establishing self-testing notes.

OLD EXAMINATIONS

Old examinations have long been a source for studying and for determining what the student knows about a particular subject. The basic theory of using old exams is that there are a limited number of questions that can be asked in any given subject. However, their use has several drawbacks:

1. Reviewing only prior examinations may not be

sufficient because you must use several years of examinations in order to completely review sufficient material. Even this does not guarantee that you will cover all the necessary information. Additionally, if there has been a recent change in the course content or if a new lecturer presented the information, the course may have a different focus. In this case, the review of prior examinations would be unproductive.

2. To use old examinations, you should cover the correct answer. Otherwise, you might unintentionally see the correct answer without truly understanding the question. Only after you understand the question should you attempt to answer it.

Another drawback is that you may become conditioned to the specific structure of the question and the noted answer. You will be learning an answer to a question worded in a particular manner. If the question is worded differently on an examination, you may have problems recognizing the correct response because of prior conditioning.

An effective method of self-testing employs a separate answer sheet for each old examination. The correct answers are eliminated from the old examination. Use a blank answer sheet when you review each question. The correct answers will now be on another sheet. After carefully reading each question, mark your answer choice on this blank piece of paper. After comparing your responses with those on the answer sheet, you will know which questions you answered incorrectly. Proceed to review this material. This is effective self- testing. In this way you can determine what you need to learn. Additionally, you reaffirm the information you know thus helping the automatization process.

Even though using old examinations has limited usefulness, they may still be helpful in several ways. It allows you to practice taking examinations. It also gives you the opportunity to ascertain the time needed to understand and answer the questions. Additionally, it allows you to practice the test-taking suggestions presented in Chapter Ten.

SELF-TESTING NOTES

The use of self-testing notes is one of the most effective and efficient ways to determine what you know and what you need to learn about a subject. It involves preparing well-organized notes derived from transcripts, personal notes, and the textbook.

The course textbook is a guide that usually presents the course material in an excellent organizational style. Each chapter has a title followed by subject headings in bold or smaller size print. Lesser headings, subordinate to the individual subject, are usually presented in a smaller size type. This text organization can be easily followed.

Use headings of the textbook to enhance organization. Use transcripts and personal lecture notes to create the self-study notes. You can include information contained in the textbook in the self-testing notes.

Mechanics

Copy textbook chapter headings on a single sheet of lined, legal size paper. (See figure 1). The chapter is entitled, <u>Muscles of Mastication</u>, from Gray's textbook on Anatomy. This outline was generated by scanning the headings in the textbook chapter. Always scan the pictures in the chapter, since they may contain valuable information. Leave space under each heading for additional information. Determine the amount of space to be left when you scan the chapter. After outlining the main headings in the chapter, list letters under each muscle indicating (O) Origin, the bone the muscle starts from; (I) Insertion, the bone the muscle inserts into; (A) Action, what the muscle does; (In) INervation, the nerves that control the muscle; and (B) Blood supply, the blood vessels that supply that particular muscle. This outline is derived entirely from the headings in the chapter.

When completed, make at least six copies of the outline. The number of copies you make determine the number of times you can self-test. If you feel the need to self-test more frequently, you may make additional copies.

Using the master copy of the outline, extract pertinent information from the textbook, transcripts, and personal lecture notes and produce an accurate summary of that particular lecture. Make all information placed on this master copy as concise as possible. When completed, the master copy of the self-testing notes should resemble figure 2. In the preparation of these notes, you are studying in a multi-sensory manner: reading and writing. If done properly, you can use these notes to study course material without again referring to the transcripts, lecture notes, and/or textbook.

MUSCLES OF MASTICATION

Masseter
  O -
  I -
  A -
  In -
  B -
Temporal
  O -
  I -
  A -
  In -
  B -
Medial pterygoid
  O -
  I -
  A -
  In -
  B -
Lateral pterygoid
  O -
  I -
  A -
  In -
  B -

Figure 1

MUSCLES OF MASTICATION
Masseter

    O - <u>Superficial portion</u> - lower border zygomatic bone
       <u>Deep portion</u> - length of zygomatic arch ----anterior end articular eminence
    I - angular region mandible - lower post. border ramus & anterior surface
    A - elevates mandible - some retraction
    In - masseteric nerve
    B - masseteric artery----internal maxillary artery

Temporal

    O - temporal fossa
    I - coronoid process, ramus, post. end alveolar process
    A -elevator, some retraction (post. fibers)
    In -temporal nerve ---mandibular nerve
    B - middle temporal artery --- superficial temporal artery, deep temporal artery --- internal maxillary artery

Medial pterygoid

    O -pterygoid fossa, medial surface lateral pterygoid plate
    I - medial surface mandibular angle
    A -elevator of mandible
    In -medial pterygoid nerve ----mandibular nerve
    B - branch of maxillary artery

Lateral pterygoid

    O -<u>inferior head</u> - outer surface lateral pterygoid plate
       <u>Superior head</u> - infra temporal surface greater sphenoid
    I - anterior surface mandibular neck - some fibers to anteromedial surface articular capsule
    A - pulls head of mandible & articular disc forward, downward & inward
    In - branch of masseteric or buccal nerve
    B - branch of maxillary artery

Figure 2

If you self-test on the Muscles of Mastication, you can use one outline sheet and attempt to fill in the information. The name of the muscle and the underlying headings [(O) origin, (A) action, etc.] will serve as a guide. You should **NEVER PUT INFORMATION ON THIS PAGE THAT YOU ARE NOT CERTAIN IS CORRECT**. Uncertainty suggests that you have not automatized the information. Place only correct information on the self-test sheet. When you place inaccurate information on the sheet, you have to "unlearn" the incorrect material and then proceed to learn the correct information, a loss of valuable time. It is not expected that you will know all the necessary information the first time a self-test is taken. The goal is to increase the amount of known information after each self-test. The final objective is to learn at least 90 percent of the necessary information before any examination.

Figure 3 represents an initial self-test. Note that some material has been filled in, but a great deal of information is missing. This is acceptable. Compare the self-test sheet to the master copy. The information on the self-test must be accurate. **Change any inaccurate information immediately**. This self-test sheet reveals what material you know and what you need to learn. Enter all the material you need to learn on the self-testing sheet. When checking the self-testing sheet with the master copy, you again review the information. The master copy is a reference. Verbalization of the information may further increase the effectiveness of the learning process.

After completing this exercise, save the master copy and discard the self-testing sheet. Depending upon several factors, (your personality, study habits, and ability to

MUSCLES OF MASTICATION
Masseter
    O -
    I -
    A - elevates mandible - some retraction
    In - masseteric nerve
    B - masseteric artery
Temporal
    O - temporal fossa
    I -
    A - elevates, some retraction, posterior fibers
    In - temporal nerve from mandibular nerve
    B -
Medial pterygoid

    O -
    I - medial surface mandibular angle
    A - elevator of mandible
    In -
    B - branch of maxillary artery
Lateral pterygoid
    O - inferior head, outer surface of lateral pterygoid plate
    I -
    A -pulls head of mandible & articular disc forward, downward & inward
    In -
    B -

Figure 3

learn), you may conduct self-testing the next evening, two days later, or when you think it appropriate. In figure 4, another self-test sheet has been used. While this sheet has more information than figure 3, it is still incomplete. Again, compare the self-testing sheet with the master, review the information placed on the sheet and fill in the missing material. You are reviewing what you know and what previously you did not know.

Save one or two self-test sheets for use prior to any examination. It is unwise to use these self-test sheets on the night before an examination, since you may not have sufficient time to learn any previously unknown information. Scanning all the master notes the night before an examination is a more effective way to reinforce the automatization process. If the self-testing process is done correctly, at least 90 percent of the needed information will be stored in long-term memory. On the night before an examination, we advise light review, followed by relaxation, and an early bedtime. Staying up late to study is usually unproductive and decreases study efficiency. The examination requires you to be alert and capable of retrieving the information.

Retain the master copy of the self-test notes and one copy in outline form for review purposes. You can use the copies for self-testing if this information is to be covered on the final course examination. Additionally, you can use both the self-test master copy and the copy in outline form in preparing for your future licensing examination.

MUSCLES OF MASTICATION

Masseter
> O - Superficial portion - lower border zygomatic bone
> Deep portion - length of zygomatic arch --- anterior end articular eminence
> I -
> A - elevates mandible - some retraction
> In - masseteric nerve
> B - masseteric artery ---- internal maxillary artery

Temporal
> O - temporal fossa
> I -
> A - elevator, some retraction by post. fibers
> In - temporal nerve ---- mandibular nerve
> B - deep temporal artery ---- internal maxillary artery

Medial pterygoid
> O -
> I - medial surface mandibular angle
> A - elevator of mandible
> In - medial pterygoid nerve ---- mandibular nerve
> B - branch of maxillary artery

Lateral pterygoid
> O - inferior head - outer face of lateral pterygoid plate
> Superior head -
> I - anterior surface of mandibular neck
> A -pulls head of mandible and articular disc forward, downward & inward
> In - branch of masseteric nerve
> B - branch of maxillary artery

Figure 4

EPILOGUE

The faculty at graduate and professional schools use examinations to determine student mastery of course content. Passing examinations is essential for success in academia. The strategies presented in this book will help you achieve this goal. Study and test-taking techniques are the difference between what is and what could be.

Clearly, there are students with learning disabilities who succeed without identification of their problem and without subsequent support services. It is also evident that there are students who fail though identified as learning disabled and given the appropriate support. Success demands more than adopting the ideas presented in this book. You have to adapt them to your own personality. For example, use a blue crayon to circle negatives on an examination rather than the recommended red pencil if it makes you more aware. Go to bed at midnight rather than 10:00 P.M. if you find this better suits your psychological make-up. Do not expect to succeed overnight. Clearly, it will take time to implement all the approaches and techniques.

General George Patton of World War II fame once said, "I would rather be lucky than smart." Luck may be very important in war, but luck has little to do with success in graduate and professional school. On occasion luck may help but it does not play a major role in academia. It is the information processed, automatized, and ready for retrieval on examinations that determines success.

Students with learning disabilities successfully completing graduate and professional schools will advance the essential elements of humankind and society. They will make significant contributions in their chosen field. The ideas presented in this book will help these students achieve their goals and aspirations. Additionally, the necessary building blocks to position these students as long time learners will be augmented by the suggestions presented in this text.

APPENDIX A

SCREENING TEST

Students assembled in a large lecture hall during dental school freshman year orientation are apprehensive, especially when their schedule indicates a screening test is to be given. No further information is available about the test. To achieve optimum results, the students must be relaxed during the screening test.

After the students are seated, the purpose of the screening test is explained. The explanation is couched in terms that lessen anxiety. They are informed that research reveals that approximately 5 percent of the students given this screening test have signs of dyslexia or other learning disabilities severe enough to affect their performance in dental school. Furthermore, if they have learning disabilities they can be helped. Identification of the problem allows the student to be exposed to methods of study that result in a more meaningfully educational experience. The ability to better process information inevitably translates into improved grades. This maximizes the possibility of the student successfully completing the dental program.

Students are given the option of not taking the screening test. They can elect to leave the lecture hall and not be penalized. (At NYUCD, no student elected not to take the screening test). The student's social security number is placed on the booklet and employed for identification purposes. The students are advised that test results are confidential. Administrators and/or faculty members are not privy to student identification. Only the Program Director and the doctoral-level psychologist scoring the examination will have a record of the test results. Notice to the administration or other college personnel of the test results will only be given with the student's approval. Their approval should be in writing.

Additionally, the students are informed that no grades are given on the screening test, only scores. Tests are carefully timed. Students, therefore, are requested to stop when time has expired. Students are reassured that no single answer has significance on the final score. The actual introduction to the screening test is presented in Appendix B, (p. 247).

Following the introduction, the students are asked if they have any questions. (Overall the questions asked at NYUCD displayed a knowledge of learning disabilities and its significance as a problem at the professional school level). After all the questions are answered, and the students are relaxed, the screening test is administered. (Students at NYUCD took the test with enthusiasm). Students may question the significance of a particular sub-test. Such questions may reflect a concern about aspects of some sub-test students feel they did poorly on and what this might suggest.

GUIDELINES

Before the screening test is given, it is important that certain guidelines be followed:

1. To accommodate a large number of students and avoid giving the screening test individually, parts of the screening test are projected. All students must be seated so they have a direct view of the screen. This is imperative, since the Berea Visual Motor Gestalt Test consists of differently shaped diagrams that have to be drawn and then redrawn from memory. If these diagrams are seen from an angle, and not directly, the student may distort the visualization of these shapes and this would adversely affect the score.

2. Students must have at least two sharpened pencils before beginning the test. These tests are carefully timed. Time lost by a student securing a functioning pencil might affect the score on that sub-test. To avoid this potential problem, each student is given two sharpened pencils when entering the testing hall. Besides the test administrator, at least two additional persons should be available to pass out replacement pencils quickly. Upper class students may be used for this purpose. All pencils must have erasers that will not smudge the paper and make the writing illegible. When the tests are scored any result that is not decipherable, especially on the spelling sub-test, will be marked wrong.

3. Students should be seated at least two seats apart. This rule is not based on the possibility of cheating. The

students are advised that an artificially high score because of cheating would be detrimental to the cheater. If students did have a learning disability and were not identified, we would be unaware of their problem and unable to help them. Students are seated two seats apart to avoid the possibility of inadvertently noticing the responses of the student in the next seat and thus be reminded of the various diagrams on the sub-test. This would negatively affect their score, especially on the Berea Visual Motor Gestalt sub-test, the number one predictor of potential difficulty in dental school.

4. All tests are carefully timed. Students are told that most of the sub-tests are designed so that few if any students would finish in the time allocated. Should they finish before the given time, they are to remain seated and not disturb the other students.

TEST ADMINISTRATION BOOKLET
(pages 185 to 201)

NEW YORK UNIVERSITY COLLEGE OF DENTISTRY
LEARNING DISABILITY PROGRAM

SCREENING TEST

Stanley J. Antonoff, DDS, FICD, FACD
Director

Administrative Time: Approximate two hours

Materials needed: Test Booklets

Directions Booklet

Pencils & erasers

Slide projector & large screen

Stop Watch

Berea Visual Motor
    Gestalt Test slides

Visual Memory for Un-Related
    Words Test slides

Staff needed: Test Administrator

Aides

Administration Notes

1.Give a brief introduction why this screening is necessary.

2.Note that the results of this test will never appear on any school records.

3.The results of this test may be helpful in maximizing the student's academic achievement.

4.The results of this test should be available in the middle of October. (Approximately six weeks after school begins).

Administration Procedures

1.Seating to be at least two seats apart.

2.Lecture or dim lights only.

3.Place on the front and back pages of each test booklet the following:

a) social security number.

b) sex.

c) student number (optional).

d) name (optional).

4. Do not look through the test booklet at any time.

5. Follow all directions carefully.

6. Anyone with a vision problem should sit in the front.

CODING

Please turn to page 2. Note the rows of boxes with numbers in them. Look at the top row of boxes, above the double lines. This is the key to the code. Each box has a number in the top part and a corresponding symbol in the lower part. Every number has a different symbol.

Now look at the body of the test. Underneath the number 2, fill in the symbol that corresponds to the number 2 in the coded line above. Beneath the next number, 1, fill in the symbol that corresponds to number 1 in the key line. Try the next few numbers as a sample. Stop at the heavy line. Fill in each box as it comes. Do not skip any! Do not just fill in the 1's or 2's.

ALLOW TIME FOR THE STUDENTS TO DO THE SAMPLES

Now, when I say go, turn the page and fill in the squares just as you have here. Fill in as many as you can without skipping any. Turn the page . . . and go!

Time: **90 seconds**

Stop

Turn to the next page, page 4.

HANDWRITING PARAGRAPH

This test, on page 4, is a simple copying task involving a single paragraph. When I say "begin," please copy the paragraph as quickly, accurately, and legibly as you can. Work until I say "stop." Ready?   Begin!

Allow two minutes

Stop

Turn to the next page, page 5. This page should be blank.

SHORT TERM AUDITORY MEMORY FOR

UNRELATED WORD SPAN

I am going to say some words to you. Listen carefully, and when I get through, write what I have said. Write the words in the same order, if you can.

Please do not start writing until I have finished saying each list completely. I will drop or lower my voice on the last word in the list.

THE EXAMINER SHOULD ENUNCIATE EACH WORD VERY CAREFULLY, READING AT THE RATE OF **ONE WORD PER SECOND**. ALLOW TIME AT THE END OF EACH LIST FOR WRITING. ANNOUNCE EACH LIST BY NUMBER . . . READY?

1. Pie   dog

2. Sand   gum

3. Hot   fork   nail

4. Can   true   air

5. Goat   east   true   pipe

6. Lamb   sock   read   two

7. Foot   doe   west   daze   word

8. Rain   tree   coast   trout   mile

9. Sad   white   nose   sail   juice   man

10. Wire   blade   hot   key   rope   water

11. Vase   boat   honey   soap   dim   bud   rain

12. Coin   pie   black   clock   hat   rope   cam

13. Frog   bone   green   wind   wood   six   plug   fan

14. South   leaf   rub   throw   bog   car   six   river

Allow time to complete the list.

Please turn to page 6.

WRITING SAMPLE

There are four essay topics on page 6 of your test booklet. Choose one topic and spend the next fifteen minutes writing a short essay, perhaps several paragraphs long. Use pages seven and eight for planning and writing in any way that you like. In order to help with your planning, I will announce when you have ten, five, and two minutes left.

ALLOW 15 MINUTES

Announce time limits as noted.

STOP

Turn to the next page, page 9.

ADDITION CODING

The test on page 9 is a coded addition task. The first line gives a code number for each of the letters a, b, c, d, and e. The second line gives samples.

Pause five seconds

You are to solve as many addition problems as possible during the time allowed. When I say start, please work as quickly as you can until I say stop. Are there any questions?

Ready?   Start!

Allow two minutes

STOP

Turn to the next page.

SHORT-TERM MEMORY FOR

UNRELATED WORD SPAN

You are now on page 10. This page should be blank. You are now going to see some words flashed on the screen. You are to observe the words during the five seconds that they are projected. After the images disappear from the screen you are to write down as many words as you can remember. Please number each line. Please do not start to write until the words are removed from the screen.

READY?

START!

Project the slides on the screen for five seconds. Allow sufficient time for writing answers.

After the last slide has been projected and sufficient time has been allowed for writing the answers, the students are asked to turn to page 11.

DICTATION

You should now be on page 11 of your test booklet and this page should be blank. I am about to read a paragraph. I will read it slowly, breaking each sentence into phrases. Listen carefully and write the paragraph from dictation as legibly and as accurately as you can. You may begin writing as soon as I start dictating. I will not repeat any phrases, so pay careful attention as I speak.

Ready?

Begin dictating each phrase slowly.

ANTICIPATING A PLACID VOYAGE / WHICH WOULD DISEMBARK THEM / ON THE FERTILE SHORES OF VIRGINIA / THE PILGRIMS / INSTEAD / LANDED ON THE STORM-DRIVEN COAST OF NEW ENGLAND.

SUFFERING PRIVATION / AND UNEXPECTED ASSAULTS / FROM THE ELEMENTS AS WELL AS FROM DISEASE / THE SCYTHE OF THE DEATH ANGEL CUT A SWATH THROUGH THEIR MIDST.

ONLY A SUPREME BELIEF / THAT THEY TRAVERSED THE MALIGNANT DEEP / IN ORDER TO SHOW THE JADED AND DECADENT SOCIETIES OF EUROPE / A BETTER WAY TO LIVE / SUSTAINED THEM THROUGH THE FIRST BITTER YEAR. / THEY IMAGINED / THAT THEIR LIVING LABORATORY OF RIGHTEOUSNESS / WOULD SO BEDAZZLE THE OLD WORLD / THAT THE NEW WORLD WOULD BE AN IRRESISTIBLE MODEL.

AS IS SO OFTEN TRUE / WHEN DREAMERS INITIATE AN ENDEAVOR / THE INITIAL GOAL IS NEVER REALIZED / BUT A USEFUL FRUIT IS BORNE ON THE DREAM-TREE THAT WAS PLANTED.

Allow the students a few seconds to catch their breath after this exercise.

SPELLING

A self-administered spelling test begins on page 12 and continues to page 13. Each word is represented phonetically in column one. A synonym or definition is given in column two. Pronounce the word to yourself. If necessary, use the definition to decide what the word is. Spell it correctly in column three. Please print or write as plainly and legibly as possible. **If we cannot read the spelled word, we will count it wrong.** Work as rapidly and accurately as you can until I say "stop."

Ready?   Begin!

Allow seven minutes.

STOP!

At this point, allowing a two minute break would be wise. Allow the students to stand in their place and relax. It is best if they do not leave the room, for this will only increase the time consumed by the break.

After the break, when the students are settled in their seats, ask them to turn to page 14.

SCANNING TEST

You are now on page 14, where you will find the scanning test. The first line says **SAMPLE.** This line has all the number 9's circled and the number 5's crossed. The next line is the practice line. Would you please circle every 9 and cross every 5 on this practice line.

Allow time to practice.

Now when I say "begin," please circle every 9 and cross every 5 that you see. Go line by line and work as quickly as you can.

READY?   BEGIN!

Allow two minutes.

STOP!

Please turn to the next page, which should be page 15.

NEW CODING

You will see the word **CODE** in large print and immediately underneath you will see a row of boxes. This is the key line to the code. Each box has a letter in the top part, and a corresponding symbol in the lower part. Every letter has a different symbol.

Now look immediately underneath this row of boxes and you will see the word **PRACTICE** in large print. Underneath the letter "M" fill in the symbol that corresponds to the letter "M" in the coded line above. Beneath the next letter "P" you should fill in the symbol which corresponds to the letter "P" in the key line. DOES EVERYONE UNDERSTAND? ARE THERE ANY QUESTIONS? Try the next few letters as a sample. Stop when you have completed this row. Fill in each box as it comes. Do not skip any! Do not just fill in the "M's," "P's," or "N's."

ALLOW TIME FOR THE STUDENTS TO DO THE SAMPLES.

Now, when I say begin, I want you to fill in the squares beneath the heavy black line just as you have done. Fill in as many as you can without skipping any.

READY?   BEGIN!

Allow two minutes.

STOP

Please turn to the next page, page 16.

BEREA VISUAL MOTOR GESTALT TEST

You are now on page 16, which should be blank.

I am going to show you a series of twelve slides. The slides have geometric figures on them. The figures are meaningless. I will show you each slide, one at a time, for five seconds. After each presentation, try to draw the figure as well as you can on page 16 of your test booklet. **DO NOT START TO DRAW UNTIL THE SLIDE HAS DISAPPEARED FROM THE SCREEN.**

You will have 30 seconds to complete each drawing. If you cannot fit all the drawings on page 16, use page 17 also.

STARTING WITH SLIDE #1, PRESENT EACH FOR 5 SECONDS. ALLOW 30 SECONDS FOR DRAWING TIME BETWEEN EACH SLIDE. AFTER THE 12TH AND LAST SLIDE IS SHOWN AND DRAWN SAY:

When you are through drawing this last design, please close your test booklet and turn it, **face up**, on the desk in front of you. You should now be looking at the cover page.

WAIT UNTIL ALL STUDENTS HAVE PLACED THEIR BOOKLET FACE UP.

Now, think back over the designs I have shown you. IN THE NEXT TWO MINUTES, TRY TO REPRODUCE, FROM MEMORY, AS MANY DESIGNS AS YOU CAN. Draw on the blank front cover of your test booklet now facing you.

BEGIN!

Allow two minutes and then say

STOP!

Please turn back to page 18.

PERSONAL HISTORY

We would like to know a little more about each of you and your educational history. On pages 18, 19, 20, and 21 are questions which will help us understand your test results in the context of your educational background. Please make a notation if English is your second language. A few phrases telling how recently you have learned English would also be helpful. When you have completed the questionnaire, you may leave.

      If you would like to speak to me at any time, I am not difficult to find and would always welcome your thoughts.

THANK YOU FOR YOUR COOPERATION AND GOOD LUCK.

THE FOLLOWING ARE THE TESTS TO BE PROJECTED ON A SCREEN AT THE APPROPRIATE TIME.

WORD SPAN   (VISUAL)

(Page 193, administration booklet)

1. Car   eat
2. Leg   bath
3. Son   canoe tune
4. Ant   tree   hate
5. Burn   dare   sand   wall
6. Comet   pin   look   road
7. Born   eight   money   eats   horse
8. Hope   best   pinch   doll   true
9. Wash   fox   grass   fun   tug   map
10. Color   born   grease book   arm   where
11. Shirt   knife   wagon   pine   get   tie   pair
12. Bud   play   water   girl   chin   right   pain
13. Boy   wish   may   bag   goats   uncle   wag hope
14. Proud   brown   pan   spare   damp   book   ape shot

BEREA VISUAL MOTOR GESTALT TEST

(Page 199, administration booklet)

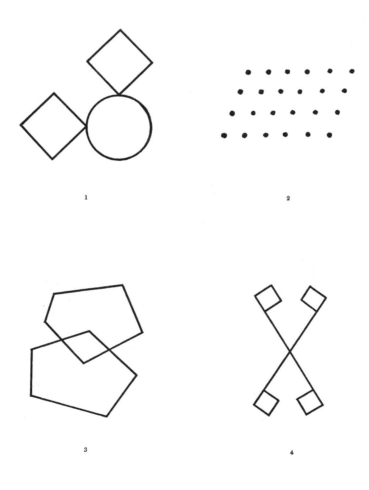

BEREA VISUAL MOTOR GESTALT TEST

(Page 199, administration booklet)

5

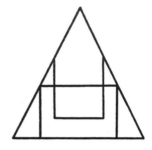

6

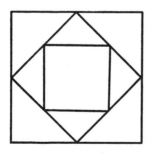

7

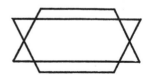

8

BEREA VISUAL MOTOR GESTALT TEST

(Page 199, administration booklet)

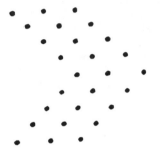

9

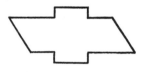

10

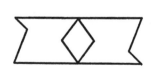

11

12

SCREENING TEST BOOKLET
(Pages 207 to 227)

NAME_____

SEX_____

CLASS # _____

SOCIAL SECURITY # _____

This **cover page** of the screening test booklet should be stapled in the upper **LEFT** hand corner. The page is blank other than the information required at the top of the page. The blank portion of this page is used for the Berea Visual Motor Gestalt Test.

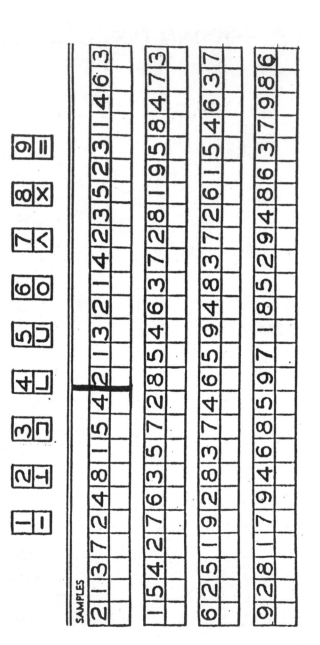

Test booklet page 2

COPYING

Zimbabwe, one of the last third-world countries to obtain its independence, became a nation on November 11, 1965. Three-fourths of its 9,186,000 people are farmers, who grow corn which is turned into "mealie porridge" ("soda"). Within its 150,804 sq. Mi. (300,580 km) territory, asbestos, chrome, coal, copper, gems, and gold are all found. There is an iron smelter at Que Que. Three-fourths of the people are black and live in the High Veld. Among the other one-fourth are many Indians and Europeans, who live mainly in towns or cities.

Test booklet page 4

This page is blank

It will be used for the Short Term Auditory

Memory for Unrelated Word Span

WRITING SAMPLE

1.Should the costs of higher education be federally funded? Why or why not?

2.Analyze and discuss the strengths and weaknesses of public transportation in a city of your choice.

3.In your opinion, what should be the primary factors taken into account by TV networks in designing the content of their programs?

4.Describe a member of your family.

PLEASE DO NOT WRITE ON THIS PAGE. USE THE FOLLOWING PAGES, PAGES 7 AND 8.

Test booklet page 6

This page is blank

It will be used for the writing sample

This page is blank.

It will be used for the writing sample.

CODE

a	b	c	d	e
5	4	3	2	1

EXAMPLES - ADDITION

$$\frac{\begin{array}{c}e\\d\end{array}}{3} \quad \frac{\begin{array}{c}d\\c\end{array}}{5} \quad \frac{\begin{array}{c}b\\e\end{array}}{5} \quad \frac{\begin{array}{c}a\\b\end{array}}{9} \quad \frac{\begin{array}{c}b\\c\end{array}}{7} \quad \frac{\begin{array}{c}c\\c\end{array}}{6}$$

a	d	b	a	a	c	d	b	c	d	e	e	c	d	e
a	b	b	e	c	a	e	a	b	a	a	b	e	d	d

e	b	d	b	b	a	a	c	e	c	b	d	d	c	e
a	c	e	a	d	b	d	c	e	d	c	b	e	b	b

a	a	e	b	b	c	c	b	a	e	c	d	a	d	b
e	a	c	b	e	c	d	b	d	e	e	a	a	d	a

d	a	a	e	e	d	a	c	b	b	b	e	e	d	a
a	d	c	e	a	e	e	b	a	c	e	a	e	e	b

b	e	a	a	d	b	d	e	c	d	e	c	a	d	b
d	e	c	a	b	b	d	b	d	a	d	a	a	b	b

a	a	c	d	b	c	d	e	e	c	d	e	e	b	d
e	c	a	e	e	b	a	a	b	e	d	d	c	c	e

Test booklet page 9

This page is blank.

It will be used for the

Short Term Memory for Unrelated Word Span

from a slide projection.

This page is blank.

It will be used for the

Dictation test.

26. grōn mature _____

27. gar en tē′ to promise performance _____

28. jest′ choor a body movement _____

29. pha nat′ i cul crazy _____

30. ka men′ di bul worthy of praise _____

31. farm′ a sist a druggist _____

32. ben e fish′ al good, useful _____

33. rich′ u ul ceremony _____

34. a koo′ sticks science of sound _____

35. wē′ sul a small animal _____

36. ek sen′ trik odd, unusual _____

37. po zes′ to own _____

38. lick′ er alcoholic drink _____

39. kal′ us tough, unfeeling _____

40. jēn′ yus exceptional intelligence _____

41. loo′ di kris absurd _____

42. plān′ tiv sorrowful _____

43. sem′ e ter ē graveyard _____

44. ō bich′ oo er ē notice of death _____

45. prar′ ē large area of grassland _____

46. scru′ pū lus upright, honest _____

47. ter′ kēz large N. American birds _____

48. prej′ u dis bigotry, hatred _____

49. ret′ o rik art of expressive speech _____

50. ek′ ste sē rapture _____

Copyright © 1985 Landmark School, Prides Crossing, MA 01965

Test booklet page 12

HOW WORD SOUNDS	DEFINITION	CORRECT SPELLING

1. yuz — employ, utilize _____

2. hell´mut — a protective head covering _____

3. few´mi gāt — to destroy pests _____

4. in ter vēn´ — to interfere _____

5. sell´cr — basement _____

6. vā´kent — empty _____

7. yōk — the yellow part of an egg _____

8. bil´ō — a swell or surge _____

9. strāt — without curves _____

10. nā´ber — one who lives nearby _____

11. dok´ter — man or woman of medicine _____

12. flōt — to be buoyant _____

13. din´jē — dirty and discolored _____

14. flor´ul — relating to flowers _____

15. ka pitch´ū lāt — to give up _____

16. awk´ū pant — a resident _____

17. spar´cul — to shine _____

18. prē sīs´ — accurate _____

19. yurn — to long for _____

20. do mān´ — territory _____

21. sē´ne rē — landscape _____

22. trans gre´shun — sin _____

23. kan´sul — to call off, annul _____

24. spawn´ser — endorse, support _____

25. nōt´i se bul — conspicuous _____

Test booklet page 13

SCANNING

Do not start until you are told to do so:

```
1  3  9  2  5  6  4  9  8  5  1  5  3  9  6  4  2  5  9  8  2  4  6  9  1
2  5  9  8  2  4  6  1  5  3  2  9  1  6  5  3  9  6  2  9  7  9  5  6  4
1  4  7  9  5  9  4  8  7  2  3  5  1  4  5  1  7  9  5  3  4  2  9  2  7
6  5  9  8  9  5  6  7  9  8  2  6  5  8  2  9  1  9  2  3  5  7  5  6  9
4  9  1  3  9  2  7  5  4  9  8  5  1  8  3  7  6  3  2  5  9  8  2  4  1
6  1  6  5  3  2  6  1  6  5  3  9  6  2  8  7  9  5  6  1  4  3  7  5  3
9  4  8  7  2  3  5  4  1  3  1  2  8  5  3  4  6  2  2  6  5  8  9  8  5
3  6  7  9  8  2  6  5  8  2  5  1  9  2  3  2  7  1  6  4  7  1  3  9  1
2  7  6  4  9  8  5  1  3  8  7  6  3  2  5  9  8  2  4  6  1  5  3  2  8
6  1  6  5  3  9  6  2  8  7  9  5  6  1  4  3  7  5  9  4  8  7  2  3  9
5  4  1  3  2  8  5  3  4  6  2  2  6  5  9  8  9  2  6  7  9  8  2  1  6
6  5  8  2  5  1  9  3  3  2  7  1  4  6  7  1  3  9  2  6  7  4  9  8  1
5  1  3  8  7  6  3  2  5  9  8  2  6  4  1  5  2  3  6  1  6  5  3  2  7
6  6  1  5  3  9  6  8  2  7  9  5  6  1  4  3  7  5  9  4  8  7  2  3  9
5  1  4  3  1  2  8  5  3  4  6  2  2  6  5  9  8  9  3  6  7  9  8  2  9
6  5  8  2  5  1  9  2  3  2  7  1  6  4  1  5  9  6  7  9  3  2  9  9  4
3  1  8  1  9  4  1  6  8  9  2  9  2  6  5  8  2  5  2  3  2  4  5  6  3
7  8  9  6  2  7  7  3  6  1  5  2  8  5  7  6  6  1  9  4  3  3  9  8  9
1  4  3  5  6  3  5  4  3  2  6  9  2  3  2  7  5  4  1  6  2  6  7  5  8
```

Test booklet page 14

-220-

CODE

M	N	O	P	Q	R	S	T	U
∧	⌋	⊥	[	—	✕	∩	⌐	·|·

PRACTICE

M	P	N	Q	R	T	M	P	R	N

STOP!

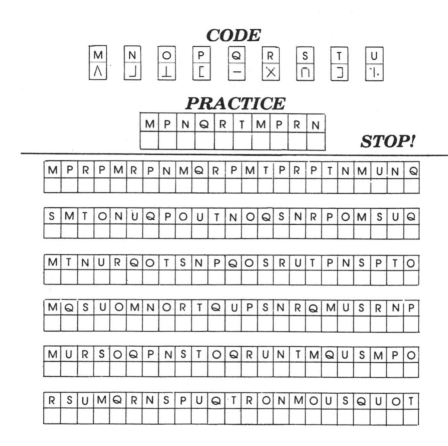

Test booklet page 15

This page is blank.

It will be used for the

Berea Visual Motor Gestalt Test

from a slide projection.

Test booklet page 16

This page is blank.

It will be used for the

Berea Visual Motor Gestalt Test

from a slide projection.

PERSONAL HISTORY

Name_____

Date of Birth_____Age___Sex___SS #_____

List Colleges Attended, Degrees Received and Major

     College   Degree   Major

_____

_____

Scores on DAT Exam   College Grade Point Average

Academic_____   Science_____

Science_____   Overall_____

PMAT_____

Father's Occupation_____

Mother's Occupation_____

Have you ever skipped a grade in school? ___Yes___No

Have you ever repeated a grade in school? ___Yes___No

     If yes, which one(s)? _____

Have you ever received remedial work or special help in reading? ____Yes____No.

     If yes, in which grades? _____

Do you have a history of any of the following? (Mark X)

____early ear infections   ____near sightedness

(Before 8 years of age)   ____far sightedness

____allergies (specify)   ____ambidexterity

____headaches while reading

Which hand do you write with? ____Left___Right

Test booklet page 18

For what subjects or fields do you have a particular aptitude? _____

Are there any subjects/fields which are particularly difficult for you? _____

What sports do you enjoy most? _____ _____

What sports do you enjoy least? _____

Do you read for fun? ___Yes ___No

    If yes, how much? _____

    What (newspapers, novels, etc.)? _____

_____

In relation to your other academic skills, how would you assess your ability to learn a foreign language?

_____

_____

Do you feel that you had more difficulty than others in your class learning any of the following skills? Please note any <u>difficulty</u>, past or present, by marking a "<u>D</u>." Mark with an "<u>S</u>" any area that was/is a particular <u>strength</u> or was developed early for your age. Mark with an "<u>N</u>" the items that are remembered as <u>neither</u> strengths nor weaknesses.

Mark   D (difficulty)   S (strength)   N (neither)

____learning the alphabet

____learning to tell time

____following or remembering verbal directions

____learning to read

Test booklet page 19

_____learning to spell
_____learning mathematical concepts
_____memorizing the times tables
_____learning script handwriting
_____learning a foreign language
_____writing compositions
_____fixing appliances or machines
_____concentrating when it is noisy
_____expressing yourself orally
_____carrying a tune
_____copying from a blackboard
_____learning any particular sports (specify) _____
_____learning dance steps
_____reading maps and diagrams
_____learning to type
_____remembering phone numbers
_____remembering historical dates or math formulas
_____organizing study time
_____keeping a rhythm
_____taking notes in lectures
_____writing an outline
_____speed reading
_____taking multiple-choice exams
_____taking essay exams
_____learning algebra
_____learning geometry

Test booklet page 20

Are the previously listed skills still problem areas for you?
___Yes ___No
>   Which ones? _____

_____

Is there a history of academic underachievement, learning difficulty, or suspected learning disability in the family?
___Yes ___No.
>   If yes, please describe (who, type of difficulty, etc.)

_____

_____

Have you or anyone in your family been diagnosed as having a learning disability, reading disability, or dyslexia?
___Yes ___No.
>   If yes, please describe (who, disability, etc.)

_____

_____

Do you have any comments about your educational history, study techniques, or future plans? _____

_____

_____

_____

THANK YOU FOR YOUR COOPERATION

Test booklet page 21

SCREENING TEST SCORING

The student's social security number, received from administration, is listed on the sheet provided. (Figure 1). The Writing Sample, Listening Comprehension (dictation) and the Berea Visual Motor Gestalt sub-tests are scored by the psychometrist. The other sub-tests are scored by student volunteers and are listed on the sheets provided. Any comments derived from the personal history are noted as well. The scoring protocol is as follows:

1. **Coding -**
      a) use key provided by placing over sub-test
      b) count the number completed
      c) subtract incorrect ones, if any
      d) the **score = b minus c**
2. **Paragraph Copying -**
      a) count the number copied
      b) add up any omissions
      c) the **score = a minus b**

For a high risk person, punctuation, capitalization, and handwriting would be reviewed. This would be done by the psychometrist.

   3. Auditory Memory -
      a) total each series and list number correct
      b) **total number correct = score**
   Homonyms are acceptable (flower - flour)
   Plural is not acceptable

SCORING SHEETS

Social Security #	Berea M	C	Coding	Paragraph Copy	Auditory Memory	Writing Sample	Addition Coding	Visual Memory	Dictation	Spelling	Scanning (6) of total	New Coding	Comments

figure 1

4. Addition Coding -
>   a) use key provided by placing over sub-test
>   b) **the number correct = score**

5. Word Span (visual memory)-
>   a) **the number correct = score**

In this sub-test the student actually saw the word, so the spelling must be exactly as presented. Plurals and homonyms are not correct.

6. Spelling -
>   a) use the word list provided
>   b) **the total of accurately**
>   **spelled words = score**

7. Scanning -
>   a) add all the 9's circled
>   b) add all the 5's crossed
>   c) **the total score = a plus b**

8. New Coding -
>   a) use key provided and place over sub-test
>   b) count the number completed
>   c) count the incorrect ones, if any
>   d) **the score = b minus c**

Note -

The Berea Visual Motor Gestalt Test was found the number one predictor in determining the "at risk" potential of a student in dental school. A perfect reproduction of the design receives a 2. A recognizable reproduction of the design receives a 1 and an unrecognizable design receives no points. With a possible perfect score of 24, many dental students received a score of six or less. These students were often diagnosed as learning disabled and had numerous problems in dental school.

APPENDIX B

DEAN'S MEMORANDUM

In view of an apparent uncertainty on the part of a number of faculty members regarding the position of the College of Dentistry Administration on the implementation of the various components of the Learning Disabilities Program in place at the College, I wish to provide clarification of that matter with this communication. It is my understanding that the following elements are the essential features of the program:

1. The population to be served by the Learning Disabilities Program consists of those students enrolled at the school who have been identified through appropriate testing procedures as being handicapped according to the definition stated in PL. 94-142.* It is generally accepted that these persons have at least average to above average intelligence.

2. The College identifies the learning disabled students through the administration of an initial screening program to entering students at the time of Freshman Orientation and a follow-up, in-depth evaluation of those students who score poorly on the screening test and who

begin to encounter academic difficulties. Experience to date has shown that four to 5 percent of recent entering classes at our dental college may be categorized as learning disabled, and it can be documented that the problem also exists at other professional schools in the United States. (1)

3. The goals of the College as they relate to learning disabled students who have been properly identified include: a) the offer of equal opportunity for such students; b) the establishment of conditions which will maximize the learning disabled student's ability to succeed, thus increasing the quality of the educational experience; and c) the retention of these students in the pre-doctoral program, if they are thus able to meet the academic requirements of the College.

4. Learning disability or dyslexia is recognized by Section 504 of the Rehabilitation Act of 1973 as a handicap for which certain academic accommodations are warranted. In accordance with the University's and the College's general policy of compliance with Section 504 as it pertains to students with different kinds of handicaps, the following academic adjustments have been offered to appropriately identified learning disabled students.

a) <u>Increased time on examinations</u>

(I) Since learning disabled students may experience difficulty in completing either written or laboratory practicals within the customary time allotted, the allowance of extra time on <u>both</u> kinds of examinations is warranted.

(II) For written examinations, the option of up to 30% additional time (e.g., 15 minutes extra for a 50 minute exam) is recommended for all learning disabled students, except for those very few individuals who may be identified by the Associate Dean for Academic Affairs (through consultation with the Coordinator of the Learning Disabilities Program or the Director of Student Affairs) as being eligible for as much extra time as is necessary. The 30% increase in time has proven adequate for most of these students and is in accord with the extra time allowance that the ADA Joint Commission on National Dental Examinations has granted to learning disabled students on the National Board Examination.

b) <u>Alternate test formats</u>

Where feasible, essay or oral exams may be preferable to multiple-choice exams for certain students in enabling them to demonstrate their knowledge. This approach is in conformity with federal legislation indicating that examinations should reflect the student's achievement in the course rather than the handicapping condition.

c) <u>Other accommodations</u>

The feasibility of any other kinds of academic accommodations, such as curriculum adjustments intended to lighten the course load, is determined on a case-by-case basis, as is also true for students with other kinds of medical problems. As with the accommodations for examinations, such requests are channeled through the

Associate Dean for Academic Affairs, who will consult with other appropriate individuals, including possible review and consent of the Executive Faculty Committee.

In conclusion, it is the opinion of the College of Dentistry Administration that the foregoing interpretation and program elements of the Learning Disability Program at the College are appropriate and fulfill both the letter and spirit of the relevant legislation. While it is true that this program goes beyond the formal level of accommodation at other dental schools and might therefore be criticized as being more than is required for the fulfillment of legal obligations, it would seem that it is in the school's and society's best interests to maximize the chances of a student with a learning disability to succeed. This presumes that the accommodations being provided do not enable the student so assisted to have an unfair advantage over his/her peers and also do not lower academic standards. Since they are provided only for students with a certified handicap and since it is expected that they would not change the knowledge or skill level required for a passing grade, these requirements would appear to be met.

* "Specific learning disability" means the disorder in one or more of the basic psychological processes involved in understanding or in using language, spoken or written, which may manifest itself in an imperfect ability to listen, think, speak, read, write, spell, or do mathematical

calculations. The term includes such conditions as perceptual handicaps, brain injury, minimal brain dysfunction, dyslexia, and developmental aphasia.

(1) Stanley J. Antonoff, personal communication.

NOTE: THE OPTION OF 30% ADDITIONAL TIME WAS LATER INCREASED TO 50%.

DIRECTOR OF STUDENT AFFAIRS' MEMORANDUM

As you know, the College of Dentistry has instituted a screening program for dyslexia or specific learning disabilities for the entering first-year class. Those students who score poorly on these preliminary tests and who begin to encounter academic problems here are recommended for further comprehensive testing. These students will receive careful evaluation to determine whether they are learning disabled.

Factors that appear to be important in determining the success of learning disabled individuals in educational endeavors include intelligence, remediation, motivation, and certain adjustments in their academic program. All these students have the intellectual potential required for a dental education, are highly motivated, and have been successful in their studies to date. With regard to academic adjustments, Section 504 of the Rehabilitation Act of 1973, with which the College of Dentistry has maintained a policy of compliance, recognizes dyslexia as a handicap for which certain academic accommodations, such as an extension of the time permitted for the completion of degree requirements, may be warranted. Since the designated functions of the Office of Student Affairs include serving as "coordinator" of Section 504 at NYUCD, it is appropriate to share with you the kinds of modifications that have been recommended for these students by the educational psychologists by whom they were evaluated and which have been offered to them, as needed, in their previous courses at the Dental Center.

(A) <u>Extra time on exams</u>: Because of their respective learning disabilities, these students may have difficulty completing exams within the customary time allotted. Thus, an important adjustment would be extra time either right before or after the official time frame, <u>both on written examinations and laboratory practicals</u>.

With regard to written exams, certain departments have responded to this need by having all students take the exam together in a separate room where additional time can be easily allotted; while other departments request that those students who need extra time at the end of the exam move to a smaller room (perhaps within the department) to complete it. In the latter case, it is important that the proctors administering the exam in different rooms know which students are entitled to extra time, in the event they request it.

(B) <u>Possible alternative means of testing</u>: For some of these students their reading disability may interfere with their ability to interpret multiple-choice questions, even though they may understand the material tested very well. In such instances, alternative forms of evaluation, such as essay or oral exams, may be helpful. This approach is in accord with federal legislation indicating that examinations should reflect the student's achievement in the course rather than the handicapping condition.

(C) <u>Drawings</u>: Drawings on an exam may pose a problem for some students in terms of their interpretation and identification of the whole or its parts. If this situation should arise, it would be helpful if the students could be quizzed orally after the exam on his understanding of such drawings and perhaps even be asked to draw certain things himself.

(D) <u>Other forms of assistance</u>: Since the particular deficits underlying their learning disability may vary from student to student, there may be other modifications or forms of assistance that may be useful on an individual basis. For example, some may need tutorial assistance for certain aspects of their laboratory work. The students have been advised to discuss their particular learning problems and needs with you, since they have developed a personal understanding of what methods of learning and evaluation are most beneficial to them.

As you realize, the accommodations these students seek are

of course not intended to give them an unfair advantage over other students, but merely enable them to demonstrate what they know. Your understanding and support will help them to achieve this goal.

Thank you for your serious attention to this matter.

MEMORANDUM REQUESTING SCORERS

TO: Previously identified students with LD & others
FROM: Stanley J. Antonoff, DDS, Clinical Professor
          Director, Learning Disability Program
RE: Screening Test Scoring

This year, the entering freshman class will be screened for learning disabilities on Monday, September 12, 1983. To expedite the results of the testing, the scoring will be done in the Schweitzer Conference room on the evenings of September 21st and 22nd starting at 4 PM. **I NEED YOUR HELP!** It would be most appreciated if you could give me this time so that we can get results quickly. In this way we can help those that need it as soon as possible.

I hope to have your help on the evenings of Wednesday and Thursday, September 21st and 22nd starting at 4 PM. If you cannot assist, please advise me.

Supper will be on me. Thank you.

DIRECTOR OF STUDENT AFFAIRS'

MEMORANDUM

TO: Department Chairpersons
           and Course Directors
FROM: Director of Student Affairs
RE: **STUDENTS' NAMES**

The dental students listed above have been diagnosed as learning disabled on the basis of the screening tests administered at the dental college during freshman orientation and subsequent comprehensive evaluation. As such, they are entitled to the academic accommodations outlined in the accompanying memorandum of April 6, 1983.* The elements of the program outlined therein were approved by the Executive Faculty Committee on April 8, 1983.

We would particularly appreciate your granting these students extra time on both written and practical examinations, when needed. For written examinations, the option of up to 50% additional time (e.g., 25 minutes for a 50 minute exam) is recommended for all learning disabled students, except for those very few individuals who may be identified, through mechanisms indicated in the accompanying memorandum, as being eligible for as much time as is necessary.

In addition, any other form of assistance or tutoring that you may be able to provide to those students who request it in the didactic or laboratory part of a course, or in the clinics, will be greatly appreciated. The students have been advised to discuss their particular learning problem and needs with you, since they have developed a personal understanding of what methods of learning and evaluation are most beneficial to them.

Thank you for your continued understanding and cooperation in this matter.

cc: Associate Dean for Academic Affairs
        Dr. Stanley J. Antonoff

* (accompanying memorandum, Appendix B, page 233)

MEMORANDUM TO STUDENTS

To: Those addressed
FROM: Director of Student Affairs

I would like you to know that the chairpersons and course directors of the departments in which you will be taking courses this year have been apprized of your learning problems and have been requested to offer you additional time to complete both written and practical examinations where needed. For written exams, you may have the option of up to 50% additional time (for example, 25 minutes extra for a 50 minute exam).

Please remember that it is <u>your responsibility</u> to check with the chairperson or course director in each department <u>well in advance of exams</u> (i.e., several days before) to determine the means by which this extra time will be afforded to you on written and practical exams: i.e., you should find out what you must do at the time of the exam to obtain this extra time.

In addition, if you feel the need for any other form of assistance or tutoring in the didactic or laboratory part of a course, or in the clinics, you should also discuss your particular learning problem and needs with these individuals. If you like, you may find it useful to show them parts of your report. I am sure you will find them cooperative and understanding.

If you need any further assistance from my office or would like to discuss any aspects of our testing program for learning disabilities, please do not hesitate to stop by to see me. In addition, you are encouraged to speak with Dr. Stanley Antonoff, Director of the Learning Disabilities Program (Department of Prosthodontics, seventh floor, Weissman Bldg., 481-5959), for suggestions on specific strategies through which you may compensate for your particular problem.

I hope you will have a successful year.

cc: Dr. Stanley Antonoff

MEMORANDUM: 1993

TO: Division Heads
FROM: Associate Dean for Academic Affairs
SUBJECT: Accommodation of Learning Disabled
               Students

Recently, I have asked faculty to make accommodations for learning disabled students in a manner somewhat different from previously. We are now asking that faculty alter examination formats, extend time for examinations beyond the 30% level, and provide extensive content tutoring.

By way of background, the 1988 Americans with Disabilities Act (ADA) provides protection for persons with disabilities and gives then assurance that they will have an "equal opportunity" to succeed. "Learning disability" is included in the list of recognized conditions qualifying for special consideration under the Act. Since this legislation was enacted, there have been several court decisions that have further defined its implementation.

The major test of the ADA is that those who have a documented disability be accorded an equal opportunity. This requires accommodation by the institution on many levels. Based on the ADA, recent court cases, and a consultation with specialists at NYU's Henry and Lucy Moses Office of Students with Disabilities (OSD), it is recommended that faculty in courses be prepared to assist students with disabilities in the following manner:

As an initial guideline, LD students be permitted 50% additional time on examinations. The needs of a particular student may indicate more time; however, this will be determined on an individual basis.

"Accommodation" includes many options, based upon evaluation of the specific learning disability of an individual student. For example, it may be determined by the Director of the Learning Disability Program that a student requires **alternative testing**; in one student's case, essay format examinations have been arranged to accommodate the disability.

Students who are diagnosed as learning disabled will be counseled by Dr. Stanley Antonoff, Director of the College's Learning Disability Program. He may also choose to involve consultants from the NYU OSD for specific support.

Cc: Dean Edward G. Kaufman
     Dr. Stanley J. Antonoff

STUDENT INTRODUCTION TO SCREENING TEST.

At the College of Dentistry, several different kinds of academic assistance for students exist. Among these different resources, is the test you will be taking today which represents an innovative approach in dental education. It is administered to freshman at our dental school and has proven helpful to us in assisting students who encounter academic problems after beginning their studies here.

It is generally understood that the pathways upon which we rely most for learning are the visual and auditory pathways, in addition to the tactile or kinesthetic sense, i.e., our sense of touch, which is especially helpful in fields such as dentistry. The test this morning is designed to assess how well you can perceive, as well as remember, information taken in through your visual and auditory channels. More specifically, the results should indicate how accurately you can read or remember abstract visual design, and how well you can understand or remember information that you have just heard. What will be tested is not your vision or hearing per se, but the ability of your brain to process or deal with information presented to you through your eyes and ears.

Each of us varies with regard to whether one channel is decidedly stronger. A certain number of individuals have severe deficits in one or both channels and have problems in reading or learning. These individuals have been termed "dyslexic" or "learning disabled" and actually represent at least 10% of the population. The problem is not a reflection of the level of intelligence and many so identified have high IQ's.

In recent years, more has become known about these problems and there is a better understanding about how to help individuals who tend to be slow learners and need more time than the average person to read and learn. By knowing where their deficits lie, they can learn to use their stronger channels more effectively and can also learn to strengthen or compensate for the weaker channels. Individuals with such problems often intuitively learn to do this over the years, especially those who have been successful academically. They can improve their coping skills further through the assistance of specialists in this area.

A few of you may already know or suspect that you have a learning problem. Or you may believe that you have poor reading comprehension or are a very poor speller. You may feel weak in certain aspects of mathematics or you may have trouble remembering information that you hear but are fine when reading it. Weaknesses such as these are by no means conclusive but merely suggest the possibility of some kind of learning problem. This type of personal background information will be requested on the form you will be using today.

This is not a test where you will receive a grade. Instead, you will receive a score on each of the sections of the test taken today. These scores will help us determine whether you may have deficits in your visual or auditory perception and memory. If you have any deficits, and if you begin to encounter academic problems, we will be in touch with you to discuss the results and try to assist you in dealing with these problems. It is important to understand that the results of these tests are only preliminary and that further comprehensive testing would be necessary for a definitive assessment of the problem.

We also wish to emphasize that the information we gain will be confidential and that it can only be used to help you in your dental studies, not to hinder you. The only reason for the existence of this testing program is to help students academically. In fact, we have found the test especially useful for dental students, since it enables us to determine whether students who are experiencing serious problems in the technical areas are just taking a while to "warm up" or whether they may have a visual perception problem that can be remediated with proper assistance.

We have also found the results valuable in advising students with no discernable learning problem about which is their best pathway for learning. This has enabled them to maximize their study efficiency by using their stronger pathway to best advantage. In view of these kinds of spinoffs, you owe it to yourself to take the test seriously and to do your best, since it may help you to identify your best study strategy and thereby enhance your ability to succeed. Therefore, if we do not contact you during the year but you are interested in reviewing the results of the test for your own enlightenment, please check with the Learning Disability Program Director.

If you are already aware that you are dyslexic or have a learning disability, or that you have always had some undefined kind of problem learning, please feel free to share this information privately with the Learning Disabilities Program Director as soon as possible. With time as precious as it is, nipping problems in the bud is one of the keys to success in dental school.

Thank you

APPENDIX C

OUTCOMES STATISTICS

TABLE 1: IDENTIFICATION OF LEARNING PROBLEMS

1. WHEN WERE YOU FIRST OFFICIALLY/FORMALLY IDENTIFIED AS LEARNING DISABLED?

  - ▸ BEFORE HIGH SCHOOL   7.7%
  - ▸ IN HIGH SCHOOL   3.8%
  - ▸ IN COLLEGE   7.7%
  - ▸ **IN DENTAL SCHOOL**   **80.8%**

2. DID EARLY IDENTIFICATION OF YOUR LEARNING DISABILITY HELP YOU IN SUCCEEDING IN YOUR FRESHMAN YEAR AND THE REMAINDER OF DENTAL SCHOOL?

  - ▸ YES   80.0%
  - ▸ NO, IT MADE NO DIFFERENCE   16.0%
  - ▸ NO, IT CREATED PROBLEMS   4.0%

3. IN YOUR OPINION, WOULD EARLIER IDENTIFICATION OF YOUR LEARNING DISABILITY HAVE MADE A DIFFERENCE IN YOUR EDUCATIONAL EXPERIENCE?

  - ▸ YES   88.5%
  - ▸ NO   11.5%

4. IN YOUR OPINION, WOULD EARLIER IDENTIFICATION OF YOUR LEARNING DISABILITY HAVE MADE A DIFFERENCE IN YOUR CAREER PATH?

- ▸ YES   28.8%
- ▸ NO   71.2%

TABLE 2: NYUCD EXPERIENCE

5. WHILE AT NYUCD YOU HAD:

	LD	NON-LD
▸ no problems learning	1.6%	84.0%
▸ problems learning related to my disability	32.3%	0.0%
▸ general problems learning	9.7%	4.0%
▸ academic problems, managed	16.1%	10.0%
▸ academic problems related to my learning disability	27.4%	0.0%
▸ academic problems not related to my learning disability	1.6%	2.0%
▸ did not want others to know I had a learning disability	11.3%	0.0%

TABLE 3: NATURE OF YOUR LEARNING DISABILITY

6. YOUR LEARNING PROBLEMS HAVE BEEN:

- ▸ primarily in the visual area   30.8%
- ▸ primarily in the auditory area   26.9%
- ▸ combination of both visual & auditory   42.3%

7. IN DENTAL SCHOOL, WHICH AREAS GAVE YOU DIFFICULTY?

		LD	NON-LD
▸	lecture courses	75.9%	60.7%
▸	laboratory courses	17.2%	21.4%
▸	clinics	6.9%	17.9%

TABLE 4: NYUCD LEARNING DISABILITY PROGRAM

8. DID YOU OFFICIALLY PARTICIPATE IN THE NYUCD LEARNING DISABILITY PROGRAM?

▸	yes	84.6%
▸	no	15.4%

9. THE NYUCD LEARNING DISABILITY PROGRAM WAS HELPFUL TO YOU WITH:

▸	getting extra time on examinations	69.2%
▸	finding out about learning	
▸	disabilities in general	61.5%
▸	finding out about my specific	
▸	learning disabilities	65.4%
▸	learning how to take tests	53.8%
▸	learning study skills	50.0%
▸	note-taking	38.5%
▸	academic subjects	26.9%

10. THE NYUCD LEARNING DISABILITY PROGRAM WAS HELPFUL TO YOU WITH:

▸	receiving support from faculty	57.7%
▸	receiving support from students	11.5%
▸	receiving support from the Dean's office	38.5%
▸	sense of self-esteem	26.9%

11. IF YOU EXPERIENCED ACADEMIC DIFFICULTY WHO HELPED YOU?

	LD	NON-LD
► director of the LD Program	65.4%	3.6%
► specific faculty member(s)	19.2%	52.6%
► chairperson(s)	11.5%	0.0%
► Dean's office	30.8%	7.1%
► other	26.9%	35.7%

12. IF YOU EXPERIENCED ACADEMIC DIFFICULTY, WHO SUPPORTED YOU?

	LD	NON LD
► director of LD program	69.2%	4.2%
► specific faculty member(s)	26.9%	50.0%
► chairperson(s)	15.4%	0.0%
► Dean's office	12.5%	19.2%
► other	3.8%	33.3%

TABLE 5: OVERALL APPRAISAL

13. ARE YOU HAPPY WITH YOUR DENTAL CAREER CHOICE?

	LD	NON-LD
► very happy	70.4%	70.4%
► somewhat happy	22.2%	18.5%
► it's OK	3.7%	7.3%
► somewhat unhappy	3.7%	1.9%
► unhappy	0.0%	1.9%

14. DO YOU FEEL SUCCESSFUL?

	LD	NON-LD
▸ very successful	69.2%	56.9%
▸ somewhat successful	26.9%	29.4%
▸ it's OK	0.0%	5.9%
▸ somewhat unsuccessful	0.0%	2.0%
▸ unsuccessful	3.8%	5.9%

15. DO YOU FEEL THAT YOUR LEARNING DISABILITY HAS HINDERED YOU IN THE PERFORMANCE OF DENTISTRY?

▸	yes	11.5%
▸	no	88.5%

16. HAS YOUR LEARNING DISABILITY HELPED YOU IN THE PERFORMANCE OF DENTISTRY?

▸	yes	23.1%
▸	no	76.9%

TABLE 6: LICENSING EXAM

17. WHEN YOU TOOK THE LICENSING EXAM, DID YOU RECEIVE EXTRA TIME FOR THE WRITTEN?

▸	yes	52.0%
▸	no	48.0%

18. DO YOU THINK RECEIVING EXTRA TIME ON
    THE WRITTEN WAS USEFUL?

    ▸   yes   85.0%
    ▸   no   15.0%

19. HOW MANY TIMES DID IT TAKE YOU TO PASS
    THE LICENSING EXAM?

		LD	NON-LD
▸	one	51.9%	72.5%
▸	two	22.2%	20.0%
▸	three	11.1%	0.0%
▸	four	11.1%	0.0%
▸	no license	3.7%(1)	7.5% (3)

20. WHICH AREA OF THE LICENSING EXAM WAS
    THE MOST DIFFICULT FOR YOU?

		LD	NON-LD
▸	written	76.9%	31.1%
▸	practical	15.4	44.8%
▸	equally difficult	7.7%	24.1%

TABLE 7: CONTINUING EDUCATION

21. DOES YOUR LEARNING DISABILITY HINDER
    YOU IN KEEPING UP WITH THE ADVANCES
    IN DENTISTRY?

    ▸   yes   11.5%
    ▸   no   88.5%

TABLE 8: RESIDENCY

22. DID YOU TAKE A HOSPITAL RESIDENCY AFTER GRADUATION?

	LD	NON-LD
▸ yes	50.0%	62.0%
▸ no	50.0%	38.0%

23. IF YOU DID NOT TAKE A RESIDENCY, WOULD YOU HAVE TAKEN A RESIDENCY IF YOU COULD HAVE GOTTEN ONE?

	LD	NON-LD
▸ yes	42.9%	52.6%
▸ no	57.1%	47.4%

24. DID YOU WORK FOR ANOTHER DENTIST AFTER RECEIVING YOUR LICENSE?

	LD	NON-LD
▸ yes	92.0%	69.6%
▸ no	8.0%	30.4%

TABLE 9: PRESENT ACTIVITIES

25. PLEASE DESCRIBE YOUR CURRENT WORK ARRANGEMENT.

	LD	NON-LD
▸ solo practice	36.7%	36.2%
▸ partnership	13.3%	11.1%
▸ space-sharing	6.7%	9.7%
▸ corporation	10.0%	8.3%
▸ working with another dentist	13.3%	19.4%
▸ other	20.0%	15.3%

26. HAVE YOU BEEN A DENTAL SCHOOL FACULTY MEMBER SINCE YOU RECEIVED YOUR DDS?

	LD	NON-LD
▸ yes	26.9%	46.2%
▸ no	73.1%	53.8%

27. DO YOU HAVE A HOSPITAL AFFILIATION?

	LD	NON-LD
▸ yes	19.2%	29.4%
▸ no	80.8%	70.6%

REFERENCES

Accardo, P., Haake, C., & Whitman, B. (1989). The learning disabled medical student. *Journal of Developmental and Behavioral Pediatrics,* 10: 253-258.

Adelman, P. B. & Vogel, S. A. (1991). The learning disabled adult. In B. Wong (ed.), *Learning about learning disabilities.* New York: Academic Press. 563-594.

Antonoff, S. J., Parks, A., Skiba, W., & Soberman, J. (1988). A survey of programs and services for learning disabled dental students. *Journal of Dental Education,* 52: 173-176.

Astin, A., Green, K., Korn, W. Schalit, M. & Berg, E. (1988). *The American freshman: National norms for 1988.* Los Angeles: University of California.

Baker, H. J., & Leland, B. (1967). *Detroit Tests of Learning Aptitude Examiner's Handbook.* Indianapolis, IN. Bobbs-Merrill.

Banks, S. K., & Guyer, K. (1995). A study of medical students and physicians referred for learning disabilities. *Annals of Dyslexia,* 45: 233-245.

Barbaro, F. (1982). The learning disabled college student: Some considerations in setting objectives. *Journal of Learning Disabilities,* 15(10): 599-603.

Bass, T. A. (1995). Being Nicholas. *Wired,* 3 (11): 146.

Blackmore, J. (1996). Pedagogy: Learning Styles, *www. cyg .net/ ~ jbalkmo/diglib/styl-a.html.*

Brown, A. L., Capione, J. C., & Day, J. D. (1981). Learning to learn: On training students to learn from texts. *Educational Researcher,* 10:14-21.

Brown, A. L. & Smiley, S. S. (1978). The development of strategies for studying texts. *Child Development,* 49: 1076-1088.

Brown University (1984). *Dyslexics at Brown.* Providence, Rhode Island.

Bruck, M. (1990). Word recognition skills of adults with childhood diagnoses of dyslexia. *Developmental Psychology*, 26:439-454.

Bursuck, Q. W., Rose, E., Cowen, S., & Yahaya, M. A. (1989). Nationwide survey of post-secondary education services for students with learning disabilities. *Exceptional Children*, 56: 236-245.

Chesler, B. (1980). *A talking mouth speaks about learning disabled college students.* Unpublished.

Clark, D. B. & Uhry, J. K. (1995). *Dyslexia: Theory and Practice of Remedial Instruction*. York Press: Timonium, MD.

Connolly, J. B. & Tully, T. (1996). You must remember this. *The Sciences,* May/June: 37-42.

Cordoni, B. (1979). Assisting dyslexic college students: An experimental program design at a university. *Bulletin of the Orton Society.* 29: 263-268.

Cordoni, B. (1980). College Programs for Learning Disabled Students, *Perceptions*, 3 (2): 1.

Cordoni, B. (1981). Services for college dyslexics. In R. Maltesha & P. Aaron (Eds.). *Neuropsychological and Neurolinguistic Aspects of Reading Disorders*. New York: Academic Press.

Cordoni, B., O'Donnell, J., Ramaniak, N., Kurtz, J., & Rosenshein, K. (1981). Wechsler adult intelligence score patterns for learning disabled young adults. *Journal of Learning Disabilities*, 14(7):404-407.

Cordoni, B. (1982). Post secondary education: Where do we go from here? *Journal of Learning Disabilities*, 15 (5) :65.

Cox, S. (1977). The learning disabled adult. *Academic Therapy*, 1(3): 70-86.

Cramer, S. C. & Ellis, W. (1996). *Learning Disabilities: Lifelong Issues*. Paul H. Brookes Publishing.

Cruikshank, D., Howell, T. H., Brinkerhoff, L. C., et al. *Journal of Dental Education*, 66 (10): 1178-1184.

Decker, T. W., Polloway, E. A. & Decker, B. B. (1985). Help for the learning disabled college student. *Academic Therapy*, 20, 339-345.

Deshler, D. D., Ellis, E. S., & Lenz, B. K. (1996). *Teaching adolescents with learning disabilities: Strategies and methods.* Denver, CO: Love Publishing.

Devine, T. (1981). *Teaching study skills, a guide for teachers.* Boston: Allyn & Bacon.

DeZazzo, J. & Tully, T. (1995). Trends, *Neuroscience*, 18, 212-217.

Durrell, D. D. (1955). *Manual for the Durrell Analysis of Reading Difficulty.* New York, NY: Harcourt, Brace and World.

Ebbinghaus, H. (1885). *Uber das Gedachtnis.* New York: Dover.

Elliot, J. L., & Thurlow, M. L. (2000). *Improving test performance of students with disabilities.* Thousand Oaks, CA. Corwin Press.

Ellis, E. S., Deshler, D. D., Lenz, B. K., Schumaker, J. B., & Clark, F. L.(1991). An instructional model for teaching learning strategies. *Focus on Exceptional Children*, 23, 6, 1-24.

Faigel, H. C.(1998). Changes in services for students with learning disabilities in U. S. and Canadian medical schools. *Academic Medicine*, 73: 1290-1292.

Fang, A. L. (2002). Utilization of Learning Styles in Dental Curriculum Development. *New York State Dental Journal.* October, 34-38.

Federal Register. May 9, 1980; 45 (92): 30937.

Federal Register. May 9, 1980; 45 (92): 30944.

Francke, A. W. & Kaplan, W. J. (1978). Easier and more productive study and desk work. *Journal of the American Optometric Association.* 1-9.

Fuchs, L. S., & Fuchs, D. (2001). Helping teachers formulate sound test accommodation decisions for students with learning disabilities. *Learning Disabilities: Research and Practice*, 16 (3): 174-181.

Ganschow, E., Coyne, J., Parks, A., & Antonoff, S. J. (1999). A 10-

year follow-up survey of programs and services for students with learning disabilities in graduate and professional schools. *Journal of Learning Disabilities*, 32:72-84.

Gajar, A., Murphy, J. & Hunt, F. (1982). A university program for learning disabled students. *Reading Improvement*, 19, 282-288.

Gerber, P. J. & Ginsberg, R. J. (1990). *Identifying alterable patterns of success in highly successful adults with learning disabilities*. US Department of Education, Office of Special Education and Rehabilitative Services, National Institute for Disability and Rehabilitation Research. Grant # H133G80500.

Gerber, P. & Rieff, H. (1994). *Learning Disabilities in Adulthood: Persisting Problems and Evolving Issues.* Boston: Andover Medical Publishers.

Goldstein, M. B. (1979). Sources of stress and interpersonal support among first-year dental students. *Journal of Dental Education*, 43(12): 625-629.

Gregg, N. & Scott, S. S. (2000). Meeting the evolving education needs of faculty in providing access for college students with learning disabilities. *Journal of Learning Disabilities*, 33:158-167.

Guyer, B. P. (1997). *The Pretenders*. Homewood, Illinois: High Tide Press.

Hasbrouck, J. (1983). Diagnosis of auditory perceptual disorders in previously undiagnosed adults. *Journal of Learning Disabilities*, 16, 206-208.

Henderson, C. (2001). *College freshman with disabilities: A biennial statistical profile*. Washington, DC: American Council on Education.

Hintzman, D. L. (1974). Theoretical implications of the spacing effect. In *Theories in Cognitive Psychology*: The Loyola Symposium (R. L. Solso, ed.). Hillsdale, New Jersey: Lawrence Erlbaum Association, 77-99.

Horn, L., & Bobbitt, L. (1999). *Students with disabilities in post secondary education: A profile of preparation, participation, and outcomes.* Washington, DC: National Center for Education Statistics.

Hurley, B. (1991). *Accommodating Learning Disabled Students in Higher Education: School's Legal Obligation Under Section 504 of the Rehabilitation Act, 32,* Boston College Law Review, 1051.

IDEA-Partnerships and CEC (2000). *Making assessment accommodations: A toolkit for educators.* Reston, VA, The Council for Exceptional children.

Jaret. P . (1992). Brain-power boosters. *Family Circle,* Aug.,52-57.

Johnson, D., & Blalock, J. (Eds.). (1987). *Young adults with learning disabilities.* Orlando, Florida: Grune & Stratton.

Johnson, D. & Myklebust, H. (1967). *Learning Disabilities: Education Principles and Practices.* Austin, TX: Pro-Ed.

Kahn, M. S.(1980). Learning problems of the secondary and junior college learning disabled student. *Journal of Learning Disabilities.* 13, 40-55.

Keyes, G. (1994). Accommodating dental students with disabilities. *Journal of Dental Education,* 58 (10): 745-751.

King, W.L., & Jarrow, J. E. Testing Accommodations for Persons with Disabilities: A Guide for Licensure, Certification, and Credentialing. *Association on Higher Education and Disability (AHEAD) Bulletin.*

Knowles, M.(1978). *The Adult Learner: A Neglected Species.* 2nd. Ed., Houston, Texas: Gulf Publishing Co.

Lee, P., & Alley, G. R. (1981). *Training Junior High Students to Use a Test-Taking Strategy,* (Research Report No. 38). Lawrence, Kansas: University of Kansas Institute for Research in Learning Disabilities.

Lyon, G. R. (1995). Towards a definition of dyslexia. *Annals of Dyslexia,* 45:3-27.

Lyon, G. R. (1996). State of Research. In Cramer, S. & Ellis, W. (Eds.), *Learning Disabilities: Lifelong Issues* (pp. 3-61). Baltimore: Brooks Publishing.

Lyons, J., Howard, K., O'Mahoney, M. & Lish, J. (1997). *The Measurement and Management of Clinical Outcomes in Mental Health.* New York: John Wiley & Sons.

Mangram, C., & Strichart, S. (1984). *College and the learning disabled student.* New York: Grune & Stratton.

Miles, T. R., Wheeler, T. J., & Haslum, M. N. (2003). The existence of dyslexia without severe literacy problems. *Annals of Dyslexia*, 53: 340-354.

Negroponte, N. (1995). Interview on the *Diane Rehm Show*, WAMU-FM, Washington, D. C.

Otis, A. S., & Lennon, R. T. (1969). *Otis Lennon Mental Ability Test.* New York: Harcourt, Brace and World.

Parks, A., Antonoff, S. J., & Drake, C. (1986, March). *Screening, diagnosis, patterns of intellectual functioning, services, and accommodations for learning disabled dental college students.* Paper presented at the Association for Children and Adults with Learning Disabilities, International Conference, New York.

Parks, A. W., Antonoff, S. J., Drake, C., Sedita, J., Weiss, I. & Daddi, B. (1982). Screening for specific learning disabilities among dental students. *Journal of Dental Education,* 46 (10): 586-591.

Parks, A. W., Antonoff, S. J., Drake, C., Skiba, M., & Soberman, J. (1987). A survey of programs and services for learning disabled students in graduate and professional schools. *Journal of Learning Disabilities*, 20 (3): 181-187.

Peronne, V. (1994). How to engage students in learning. *Educational Leadership,* 51: 11-13.

Perkins, D. & Blythe, T. (1994). Putting understanding up front. *Educational Leadership*, 51: 4-7.

Phillips, S. E.(1993). *Testing Condition Accommodations for Disabled Students*, 80 Educ. L. Rep. 9.

Rawson, M. (1977). Dyslexia as adults: The possibilities and the challenge. *Bulletin of the Orton Society*, 27: 193-197.

Raymond, L. & Brinckerhoff, L. (2002). Medical students at risk: A multi disciplinary approach to service delivery. *Perspectives*, 28 (2): 35-38.

Reiff, H. B., Gerber, P. J. & Ginsberg, R. (1997). *Exceeding Expectations: Successful Adults with Learning Disabilities*. Austin, Texas. Pro-ed.

Rhodes, P. & Swedlow, D. (1983). A dental student tutor program. *Journal of Dental Education*, 47(5):325-328.

Roediger, H. L. (2002). *Memory (psychology)*. Microsoft Encarta Online Encyclopedia. Http://encarta.msn.com.

Rosebraugh, C. J. (2000). Learning disabilities and medical school. *Medical Education*: 54:994-1000.

Rottinghays, K. & Wilds, W (1992). Case Comment, Wynne v. Tufts University School of Medicine, 19, *Journal of College & University Law*.

Runyan, M. K. (1991). The effect of extra time on reading comprehension scores for university students with and without learning disabilities. *Journal of Learning Disabilities*, 24(2): 04-108.

Sachs, R. H., Zullo, T. G., & Close, J. M. (1981) Concerns of entering dental students. *Journal of Dental Education*, 45 (3): 133-136.

Sears, J. D.(1988). Learning disabilities, post secondary education and Section 504 of the Rehabilitation Act of 1973. *Law and Psychology Review*, 12: 61-78.

Sedita, J. (1980). *Section 504: Help for the learning disabled college student*. Prides Crossing, MA: Landmark Foundation.

Shapiro, J., & Rich, R. (1999). *Facing learning disabilities in the adult years*. New York: Oxford University Press.

Shaywitz, S. E., & Shaw, R. (1988). The admissions process: An approach to selecting learning disabled students at the most selective colleges. *Learning Disability Focus*, 3: 81-86.

Simpson, E. (1979). *Reversals.* Boston: Houghton-Mifflin.

Skinner, L., Gillespie, P., & Balkam, L. (1997). Adults who learn differently: Help through a volunteer literacy program. *Annals of Dyslexia,* 47: 185-202.

Steinberg, J. L. (1996). *Learning Disabilities: Information and Resources.* Prides Crossing, Mass.: Landmark Foundation

Thurlow, M. L., Elliot, J. L., & Ysseldyke, J. E. (1998). *Testing students with disabilities: practical strategies for complying with district and state requirements.* Thousand Oaks, CA. Corwin Press.

Thurlow, M. L., & Johnson, D. R. (2000). High-stakes testing of students with disabilities. *Journal of Teacher Education*, 54 (4): 305-314.

United States Public Law 94-142, The Education for All Handicapped Children Act, 1978.

United States Public Law 93-112, The Rehabilitation Act of 1973. Section 504.

United States Public Law 101-336, The Americans with Disabilities Act, 1990.

United States Public Law 102-119, The Individuals with Disabilities Education Act, 1990.

Vacca, R. T. (1998). Let's not marginalize adolescent literacy. *Journal of Adolescent & Adult Literacy*, 41: 604-609.

Vogel, S. (1982). On developing learning disabilities college programs. *Journal of Learning Disabilities*, 15 (9): 518-528.

Vogel, S. (1986). Levels and patterns of intellectual functioning among LD college students: Clinical and educational implications. *Journal of Learning Disabilities*, 19 (2): 71-79.

Vogel, S., & Adelman, P. (1992). The success of college students with learning disabilities. *Journal of Learning Disabilities*, 25 (7): 430-441.

Vogel, S., & Forness, S. R. (1992). Social functioning in adults with learning disabilities. *School Psychology Review*, 21: 375-386.

Vogel, S., & Adelman, P. (Eds.). (1993). *Success for college students with learning disabilities*. New York: Springer Verlag.

Walters, J. A., & Croen, L G. (1993). An approach to meeting the needs of medical students with learning disabilities. *Teaching and learning in medicine*, 5: 29-35.

Ware, J., & Hays, R. (1988). *Methods for measuring patient satisfaction with specific medical encounters*. Medical Care, 45: 122-128.

Weaver, S. (1993). *The validity of the use of extended and un-timed testing for post secondary students with learning disabilities*. Doctoral Dissertation.

Wechsler, D. (1955). *Manual for the Wechsler Adult Intelligence Scale:* Psychological Corporation, New York, NY.

Weintraub, P. (1992). Total recall: Ways to improve your memory. *American Health*, March, 77-78.

West, T. G. (1997). *In the Mind's Eye*. Amherst, NY: Prometheus Books.

Williams, J. (1990). *The organization of study skills*. Dallas, TX: About Class.

Winkler, D. A. (2000). Turning differences into advantages. *Perspectives*, Spring, 26 (2).

Wittrock, J. W. (1983). Remediating clinical problems. *Journal of Dental Education,* 47 (5): 340-343.

Yin, J. C. P., Del Vecchio, M., Zhou, H., & Tully, T. (1995). CREB as a memory modulator: Induced expression of a dCREB2 activator isoform enhances long-term memory in Drosophilia. *Cell,* 81: 107-115 .